Around Hylton Castle

by

Alan Brett

Acknowledgements

Richie Ankers, Bobby Bland, Ann Bruce (née Moss), Harry Bruce, Andrew Clark, Phil Curtis, Gareth Huw Davies, Billy Dent, Billy Donkin, *Evening Chronicle*, *Football Echo*, Peter Gibson, Phil Hall, Alex Handy, *The Journal*, Derek Laidler, Kath McIvor, Peter Martin, Monkwearmouth Library, George Nairn, Newcastle Central Library (Local Studies), Tony Nesbit, Northeast Press, Pat O'Brien, Geoff Pearson, Les Purvis, *Radio Times*, Michael Reid, Stan Reid, Jeff Richardson, Martin Routledge, George Semens, Sunderland Central Library (Local Studies), *Sunderland Echo*, Ashley Sutherland, Jack Stephenson, Keith Stevenson, Michael Stephenson, Alan Tedder, Tyne and Wear Museums (Sunderland Museum and Art Gallery, Jim Weatherill, Billy Wood, Ian Wright, John Yearnshire.

Bibliography

James Burnett *History of the Town and Port of Sunderland* 1830
George Garbutt *History of Monkwearmouth, Bishopwearmouth and Sunderland* 1819
Peter Gibson *Southwick-on-Wear Volume 4* 1996
Geoffrey E. Milburn and Stuart T. Miller *Sunderland River, Town and People* 1988
William Cranmer Mitchell *History of Sunderland* 1919
Taylor Potts *Sunderland: A History of the Town, Port, Trade and Commerce* 1892
Raymond Selkirk *The Piercebridge Formula* 1983
Alfred Spencer *Life of Harry Watts* 1911
Jeremiah William Summers *The History and Antiquities of Sunderland* 1858
Robert Surtees *The History and Antiquities of the County Palatine of Durham* 1816-1840
William Proctor Swaby *The Short History of the Castle, Family and Estates of the Hiltons of Hilton Castle in the County of Durham* 1884
John Thompson *Old Monkwearmouth & Its Surroundings* 1892

First published 1997

The People's History
Suite 1
Byron House
Seaham
Co. Durham
SR7 0PW

ISBN 1 899560 40 8

Newspapers & Journals

Football Echo
Newcastle Courant
Radio Times
Sunderland Echo
Sunderland Herald
Sunderland News & North of England Advertiser
Sunderland Weekly Echo

Reports & Minutes

Sunderland Annual Report of the Medical Officer of Health 1936
Sunderland Council Minutes 1930-1933
Southwick Area Plan 1967

Contents

INTRODUCTION

While the historic Hylton Castle provides the starting point for this book a large part features the surrounding estates which have never been covered before. People might find it hard to imagine the picturesque North Hylton of today as a bustling industrial centre but this was the case in the last century. Not all Castletowners might know their village was built to accommodate the workers of the Wear Rolling Mills in 1870. The land on which the housing estates were built also have a story to tell. Roman discoveries have been found at Carley Hill where the lime quarries were worked for centuries.

Marley Pots was an example of a pre-war council housing project. Like the estates that were to follow after the war they provided a new start for people from the overcrowded areas of Sunderland. Some of these like Red House, Town End Farm, Witherwack all bear the names of the farms upon which they are built. Few might realise Downhill was the scene of a battle in the English Civil War.

In recent years the estates surrounding Hylton Castle have undergone remarkable change. Huge sums of money have been poured in to renovate housing and improve amenities on the estates. The area between North Hylton Road and the riverside has also undergone radical changes in recent years. Firms like Ericsson and Olin Mathieson are no longer in the post-war factories there but new industries have taken their place. Amidst this industrial regeneration space has still been kept for the Nature Reserve at Timber Beach.

For more than a decade cars have been coming off the production line at the Nissan plant but the airfield it replaced also has a long history. The Royal Flying Corps and then later the RAF were based at the aerodrome. In peacetime the airfield used to stage the Airshow which is now held on the seafront.

The estates have produced surprisingly large numbers of professional footballers and boxers. This reflects the almost exclusively working class nature of the area. The traditional means of escape for young boys has been these professions. However, the area can also boast others who have made their mark in different fields. Richard Bull is the Fire Chief of Tyne and Wear, Sheila Allen is a top athlete and Albert Anderson is author of a number of successful books.

Numerous sources have been used in compiling this book. These include: Council Minutes, Census (1831-1891), local newspapers, maps and reports. The memories of residents and visitors provides a personal touch to the story of *Around Hylton Castle*. Former Air Cadet Jim Weatherill recalls the day when a Flying Fortress paid an unscheduled visit to Usworth Airfield during the war.

HYLTON CASTLE

Hylton Castle in winter 1990.

The Hyltons of Hylton Castle

There is some uncertainty as to exactly when the Hylton (Hilton) family first lived on Wearside. There are legends that they were Vikings who settled on the banks of the Wear a thousand years ago. The first firm evidence of their presence comes in an agreement between Romanus de Hylton and the Prior of Durham in 1157. This allowed a chaplain to officiate at the chapel of Hylton.

Less than a decade later the Hylton estate was described as being 'long established' so it is fair to assume the Hylton lands could go back to the Norman Conquest in 1066.

Whatever the date they arrived the Hyltons prospered for centuries at Hylton Castle. In the late 12th century Alexander of Hylton was described as a 'Baron of the Bishopric.' The Hyltons distinguished themselves in battle in the cause of the crown over the years.

Major problems for the Hylton family began in 1641 with the death of Henry Hylton. His will left the bulk of the Hylton estate in the hands of the Lord Mayor of London and trustees for 99 years. This charitable gesture was followed by long and costly litigation. Then almost immediately the Hyltons were in more trouble as they became embroiled in the Civil War on the King's side. Ending up on the losing side was a further strain on the Hyltons' resources.

After the last Baron of Hylton died in 1746 his sister's son Sir Richard Musgrave inherited the estate. Four years later Musgrave was granted an Act of Parliament to put the 5,600 acre estate up for sale. At this time the estate brought in £3,000 in rents annually. Hylton Castle and its grounds were bought by Mrs Bowes, widow of George Bowes of Streatlam and Gibside. This later passed on to the Earl of Strathmore.

In 1863 William Briggs bought Hylton Castle and proceeded to refurbish it in his own style. The castle passed down through the Briggs family until the turn of the century. After the death of Colonel Charles James Briggs the family left Hylton Castle.

An engraving of Hylton Castle in 1728 by Samual and Nathaniel Buck.

Mail Coach

In *Old Monkwearmouth & Its Surroundings* John Thompson recalled how the mail coach used to pass the Hylton estates early in the last century. 'It was a lovely landscape then, viewed from outside of the mail coach. Hylton Castle was one of the first objects that caught the traveller's eye.'

Right: An advert from the *Newcastle Courant* of 12th July 1800.

COUNTY of DURHAM.
To be LET,
For such a Term of Years as may be agreed upon,
HYLTON CASTLE, with the Privilege of killing Game over an extensive Manor.

The Tenant may be accommodated with any reasonable Quantity of Land at May-day next; and the Castle, which contains many capital Rooms, and will suit a large Family, may be entered upon immediately.

Hylton Castle is situated on the Banks of the navigable River Wear, in the Vicinity of Sunderland, and about seven Miles from Newcastle upon Tyne, both capital Markets. The Lambton Hounds are kept in the Neighbourhood, and a Pack of Harriers within a very short Distance.—For Particulars enquire of Messrs Farrer, Lacey, Headman, and Wall, Bread-street-hill, London; or of George Burdon, Esq. Newcastle upon Tyne.—July 10, 1800.

Turner at Hylton Castle

Above: An engraving of Hylton Castle from a picture by J.M.W. Turner. One of England's most celebrated artists was commissioned by the Earl of Strathmore in 1817 to produce a landscape of the castle and its grounds. The original watercolour was auctioned at Sotheby's in 1984. An anonymous buyer paid £68,000 for the work.

Right: Joseph Mallord William Turner who the Earl persuaded to come to Hylton Castle.

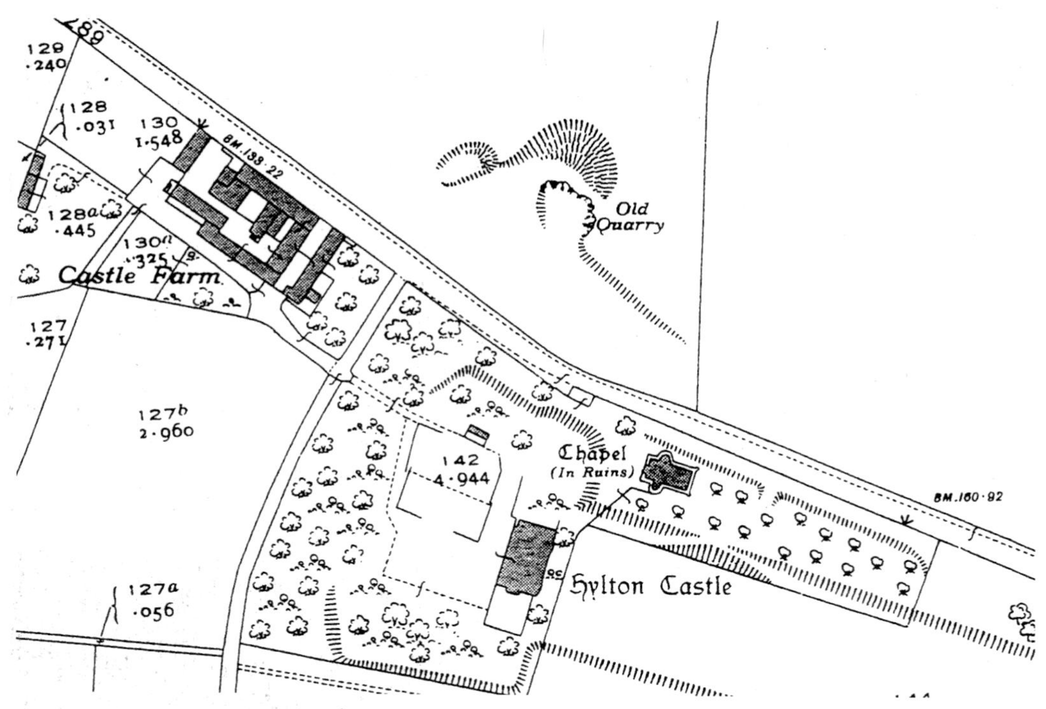

A map showing Hylton Castle and Castle Farm which stood opposite. The Health Centre now stands on the site of the farm.

Hylton Castle and St Catherine's Chapel early this century. The 1841 Census recorded John Wood, his wife Annabella and his six children, living at the castle. Wood was running a school at the castle and boarding there at this time were: three male teachers, 22 male students, a governess and four girl pupils.

Hylton Castle Boarding School

In the 1840s the chapel of Hylton Castle was used as a boarding school by the Reverend John Wood. Wood was a Scotsman who ran schools at Hendon Lodge and Broad Street (Roker Avenue) for the children of the town's well off. The majority of children at this time did not attend school.

Right: An advert for Hylton Castle Boarding School from the *Newcastle Courant* of 10th July 1840.

HYLTON CASTLE BOARDING SCHOOL,
CONDUCTED BY THE REV. JOHN WOOD, LL.D.,
(FORMERLY OF HENDON LODGE),

WILL be opened for young gentlemen, on Monday the 20th of July, 1840. Terms of board and education, &c. may be had upon application to Dr. WOOD.

References to Clergymen of the Established Churches, both in England and Scotland, will be given, if required.

N.B. Hylton Castle, formerly the celebrated residence of the Barons of Hylton, now the property of John Bowes, Esq. M.P., for beauty of scenery, salubrity of climate, and admirable adaptation for a boarding school establishment, if equalled, is not surpassed, in the kingdom.

Hylton Castle, near Sunderland, County of Durham, July 9th, 1840.

Joseph Swan

The most famous pupil of John Wood's Hylton Castle School was undoubtedly Joseph Swan - inventor of the incandescent electric lamp.

Born at Pallion Hall on 31st October 1828 young Swan studied at Hendon Lodge before moving up to the school at Hylton Castle. He left the school to take up an apprenticeship as a chemist and druggist. His spare time was devoted to scientific experiments. Swan made a number of important discoveries in the field of photographic development before unveiling his electric filament lamp to the world in 1879. At the same time in America Edison was working on exactly the same invention. The pair later joined forces and formed the Edison and Swan United Electric Light Company.

A photograph of Joseph Wilson Swan taken a few years after his Hylton Castle schooldays.

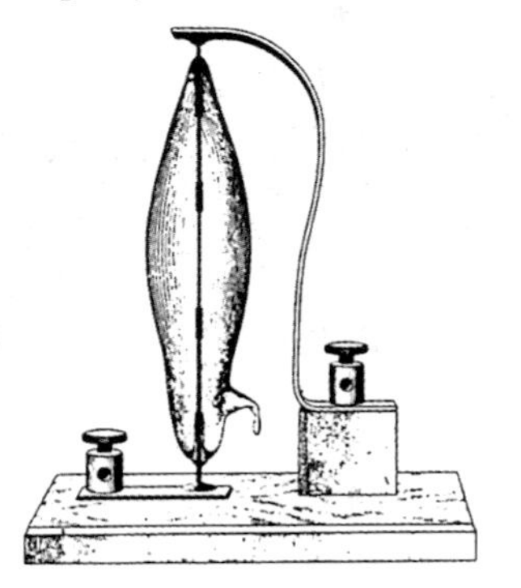

Left: The lamp Swan first demonstrated at the Literary and Philosophical Institute in Newcastle on 3rd February 1879.

The Landed Gentry

The Castle

Today's castle dates from around 1400 but there is evidence of earlier structures on the site. Over the years various wings were built and later demolished. In the 1950s the Ministry of Works took over and totally gutted the inside of the castle, knocking down all the floors and the roof.

Baron's Quay

Baron's Quay was named after the Barons of Hylton who used to have their barges at the riverside there. The 1861 Census records a keelman called Robert Wilson living at Baron's Quay.

A road which ran from the Quay up to Hylton Castle still survives today.

Chicken for Christmas

Every Christmas in the 1750s the head of the Hylton family received a hen from each tenant on his estate.

At one time the Hylton family owned all the land that could be seen from the battlements of the castle.

Greyhounds: Bringer of Death

There is a legend that the Hyltons used to know when a Baron was going to die. It was said a greyhound always conveyed the news of imminent death of the head of the family. William Swaby recalled how a greyhound entered the dining room of the last Baron of Hylton. The dog went straight over to the Baron and laid its head on his knee. The Baron stood up and said 'I shall die soon; this dog always comes to warn the head of the house before he dies.'

Greyhounds: Bringer of Fines

On 11th June 1853 four men appeared at Sunderland Police Court charged with poaching on the Hylton estate. The men were hunting hares with two greyhounds and three lurches on a Sunday in the previous month. They were caught with two hares while heading towards Boldon. Each man was fined £2 or thirty days imprisonment.

Time Team at Hylton Castle

In 1994 the prize-winning television programme *Time Team* came to Hylton Castle. Tony Robinson & Co spent three days surveying the castle and its grounds.

Working with archaeologist Steve Speak from Tyne and Wear Museums, the team dug trenches and carried out an underground survey in the castle grounds. They found the remains of settlements covering different periods on the site. They discovered the foundations of a medieval banqueting hall and Elizabethan gardens. A number of imported ceramic floor tiles were discovered indicating the occupants were wealthy and of high standing.

After the *Time Team* discoveries it is hoped to recreate features beside the castle such as an Elizabethan Garden and an ornamental lake.

Tony Robinson is up to his knees in bones in a medieval butchers' back yard. A group of 9-year-olds, nattily kitted in the Sunderland football strip, edge close. "Children, please don't stand on the edge of the trench or Phil goes mad." Archaeologist Phil Harding, leaning on his spade like the grave digger from *Hamlet*, gives them a theatrical scowl.

"Now Phil, what's that one there?" Robinson, whose job on *Time Team* it is to pose the layman's questions, points to a jawbone gaping out of the substratum. "Bit of old cow, I shouldn't wonder," says Phil Harding, the team's resident digger, a bluff Wiltshireman with a voice like butter freshly churned on the Marlborough Downs. "No it's not, it's a wolf," pipes up an unreformed romantic from the encircling Roker Park youth wing.

Gareth Huw Davies
Radio Times

'An Agreeable Place of Recreation'

The idea of turning the Hylton Castle grounds into a pleasure garden is not new as seen by a report from *The Sunderland News and North of England Advertiser* of 14th February 1852:

HYLTON CASTLE — in the vicinity of the old castle at Hylton, a plot of land, to the extent of 12 acres, is about to be laid out as public gardens and the large room in the castle will be converted into a ball room. Hylton Castle, connected as it is with so many old associations, is situated on the banks of the Wear, about three miles from this town, and will be an agreeable place of recreation, as it can be readily approached either by land or water.

In recent years work has started on improving the castle's grounds. An avenue of trees and flower beds are a couple of the new features.

The New Order

In the summer of 1863 Hylton Castle was bought by local businessman William Briggs. Briggs was a timber merchant, shipbuilder and shipowner who built his business up into a thriving concern. This was helped along the way by doing Government work during the Crimean War. His Pallion shipyard built a number of gunboats to help the war effort. He was later joined in the firm by his sons.

After acquiring his very own castle where he could be lord of the manor, he proceeded to alter and restore the castle to what he saw as its former glory. He had the modern wings demolished bringing the castle down to more 'habitable dimensions.'

The Colonel also involved himself in the local community. He became a councillor and fought to bring gas and electricity to Castletown.

Right: Hylton Castle in the early years of this century in its final days of habitation.

Colonel Briggs

William's son Colonel Charles James Briggs of the Durham Light Infantry inherited Hylton Castle.

In 1953 in a letter to the *Echo* Mansfield Gibson recalled:

'Col. Briggs was a very likeable man. If you met him on the lonely road from Southwick to Castletown the Colonel would not pass without a pleasant greeting. He was well known in Southwick as his grounds were always available for any charitable organisation arranging a fete. On those very enjoyable occasions the Colonel would come among the crowd and chat with all and sundry. I have had some happy times in the Castle grounds.'

The Briggs Family

In 1871 thirty-six-year-old Charles Briggs farmed 685 acres on his estate at Hylton Castle. He employed 12 men and 12 women. Ellen Cobden a cook from Sussex and Deborah Hall a housemaid from Boldon stayed at the castle. Charles lived in the castle with his wife Sarah (34) from Surrey and children Ada (9), Annie (8) Douglas (6) and Charles (5). The Briggs' went on to have a total of 12 children.

Two Weddings and a Funeral

The Rich Man in his castle
The poor man at his gate.
God made them, high or lowly,
And order'd their estate

The wedding of Annie Briggs, daughter of the Colonel, took place at St Margaret's Church on 29th July 1890. The groom Mr Goldthorp was from a wealthy family of Yorkshire mill-owners. The wedding was a big occasion with the tenants on the Hylton Castle estate treating the day as a holiday. Horses from the five farms on the estate were paraded before guests staying at the castle. Prizes were given for the best groomed and harnessed horses with Mr Metcalfe of Park House Farm winning and Mr Scott of Town End Farm coming second.

The following day the *Sunderland Daily Echo* published a long list of wedding presents which were on display at the castle. These included: from the tenantry of the Hylton Castle estate - large bronze clock and figures and silver hot water jug; from employees of Hylton castle estate - silver tea tray; from domestic servants - brass and oak clock; from members of Southwick Conservative Club - oak writing desk; and from the groom's mill hands - silver tea and coffee service and silver-plated afternoon tray.

Colonel Briggs had St Margaret's Church at Castletown built in memory of his parents in 1874. It cost £2,500 to construct and the vicar was paid £275 a year.

Two years later the Briggs' eldest daughter Ada was married to Claude Valentine Gee. The groom was vicar of Castletown Parish Church. As well as gifts from family and friends the tenants on the Hylton estates again contributed to the occasion. The working people of the parish made a finely embroided altar frontal which was used at the ceremony. This had been made by a group of girls in their spare time. The *Echo* said many of these 'labour in the fields all day and none have undergone any special training for such delicate work.' By the time the girls were back working in the fields the newlyweds were on honeymoon on the Continent.

Colonel Briggs died on 15th October 1900 after a long illness. The Colonel left instructions that he wanted a quiet funeral but large crowds still gathered to pay their last respects. Family, friends, tenants, servants and farmhands walked from the castle to St Margaret's Church for the service. Reverend Gee, who had married the Colonel's daughter 8 years before, met mourners as they entered his church. As the cortege made its way to Sunderland Cemetery the road from Castletown to Southwick was lined by large crowds.

The Colonel's death was not only to signal the end of the Briggs' era at Hylton Castle but also the beginning of the castle's steady decline.

On 15th and 16th November 1904 the auction of furniture and contents of Hylton Castle took place. Horse drawn carriages were laid on for serious buyers and the curious alike. These ran between Southwick Tram Terminus and the castle at 3d a trip.

The lots included Sheraton furniture, a 7ft tall white marble statue by Lombardi, Sevres vases, a billiard table, a bagatelle table and a horse and carriages.

Among the more unusual articles for sale were stuffed birds, foxes and rabbits and a skull in a case.

Charlie Buchan at Hylton Castle

As soon as war was declared in August 1914 Sunderland AFC star Charlie Buchan wanted to join up. However, League football continued until the following April. When the time came around he joined the Grenadier Guards. After serving on the Western Front at the Somme, Cambrai and Passchendaele he returned to join an Officers' Cadet School at Catterick Camp in 1918. From here he was posted to Hylton Castle with the Sherwood Foresters.

After the war Buchan returned to Roker Park and carried on where he had left off as one of Sunderland's greatest goalscorers.

England international Charlie Buchan in Sunderland colours and in uniform during the First World War.

The Army camp set up in Hylton Castle's grounds during the First World War.

Early this century Hylton Castle was a popular destination for people from Sunderland. It gave families the chance to have picnics in the fresh air. It was also an ideal location for local schools and scout troops to set up camp. Although it was only a few miles from the centre of Sunderland the land around Hylton Castle provided open spaces for 'townies' to escape to.

Right: Hylton Castle before undergoing radical change.

In 1950 the Ministry of Works took over guardianship of Hylton Castle. The following year work started on the building after decades of neglect.

Hylton Castle Housing Estate

Fresh Start

The first tenant on Hylton Castle Estate was John Richardson and family. The Richardsons left Cooper Street in Roker to take possession of 2 Canterbury Road in May 1953.

Although at this time the estate was not yet known as Hylton Castle but only as the new Castletown estate.

It's A Wonderful Life

One of the earliest residents of Hylton Castle Estate was Mary Turnbull. She soon saw improvements in her children's health after moving to her new home in Cotswold Road. 'Before we came here they used to get a terrific number of colds, now they are free from that sort of thing. We like it out here - it's wonderful.'

It's not every housing estate that can boast a castle at the end of the street.

Three teenage girls pose in the 1960s with the castle in the background.

Hylton Castle

By the mid-1960s there were 1,921 houses at Hylton Castle with plans for a further 56 to be built. The estate's population in June 1966 stood at 7,799. The average number of people per dwelling was 4.06.

For decades the Hylton Castle Arms has been a favourite watering hole for the estate's residents. The pub has recently been renamed the 'Hylton Castle'.

Sheriffs of Hylton Castle

When the new estates were going up to the west of the town after the Second World War policemen were housed in the communities. These officers were known as sheriffs. Stan Reid and Malcolm Shewan were the first sheriffs of Hylton Castle.

Police stations were built with adjoining houses on either side where the men and their families lived. There were doorways from both houses directly into the 'police office'. One man was on duty during the day and the other at night.

Stan recalled how he had to travel everyday to the police box near the roundabout at Southwick to report for duty. He would then call into Jimmy Connor's shop as part of his routine.

Stan Reid and family. Stan was on the estate from 1954 until 1979

Malcolm Shewan and his children outside the police house at Hylton Castle.

The police house at Hylton Castle is now a private residence.

Hylton Castle Library opened in August 1967 at a cost of £53,600. This modern designed building housed a stock of 18,000 books on its opening day.

Right: Kath McIvor (née Wood) keeps a couple of youngsters amused in the snow outside the library in the 1980s.

Butcher's Boy

I had a Saturday job at Walton the Butchers opposite where Hylton Castle Library is today. I started in 1962 when I was nine years old. I used to deliver orders on a bicycle with a large basket on the front. One day, not long after I had started, I was speeding along when the bottom of my trousers got caught in the chain. I went flying over the handle bars and split my chin open. A lady who rushed over to help was no doubt relieved to find the blood and gore on my face was mostly from a client's mince delivery. My trousers were still stuck in the chain and had to be cut free. I needed 11 stitches in the wound and still bear the scar to this day. The incident did not put me off and I remained in the job for another four years.

Billy Wood

Cauld Lad of Hylton

The Cauld Lad of Hylton is one of the most famous legends in the North East of England. The ghost of a boy is said to haunt the castle. This is said to be the spirit of a stable boy killed by a Baron of Hylton who flew into a rage. The Baron was said to have hidden the body in a nearby pond.

There is on record the death of a boy killed by a member of the Hylton family almost four centuries ago. On 3rd July 1609 an inquest was held on Robert Skelton, who had been accidentally struck by a point of a scythe wielded by Robert of Hylton. Robert had been cutting grass when the unfortunate incident occurred. Three days later he was granted a free pardon by the Bishop of Durham.

Right: The cover of a book about the Cauld Lad published in the last century.

Below: The legend lives on today at Hylton Castle in the form of the Cauld Lad public house.

Health Centre

A Health Centre was built on the site of Hylton Castle Farm around 1961. This still serves thousands of people on the neighbouring estates.

Below: A children's party celebrating the Queen's Jubilee in 1977.

Hylton Castle Workmen's Club

In 1954 there were calls for a club at Hylton Castle but things never got off the ground. Then in May 1957 at a meeting at Castle View Junior School plans for a club were finalised. With the backing of a brewery a site at Cricklewood Road near Ferryboat Lane was chosen. The Mayor and Mayoress were at the official opening on 10th November 1958.

The club started with a membership of 250 with a further 150 on a waiting list. The first chairman of Hylton Castle Workmen's Club was John Krieger.

The shops at Chiswick Square in 1976.

Hylton Castle's David Rush was a prolific goalscorer for Sunderland Primary Boys side. His footballing education continued at Castle View School. After leaving school he had a brief spell with Notts County before returning to join his hometown club. The highlight of his Roker career was an FA Cup Final appearance at Wembley in 1992. David later played for Oxford and York City.

One of the finest boxing prospects in the country comes from Hylton Castle. Robbie Bell won the Golden Gloves in 1993, which is regarded as the amateur championships of Great Britain. In a glittering amateur career he also represented England before turning pro.

Fire Chief

Richard Bull, Chief Fire Officer of Tyne and Wear Metropolitan Fire Brigade, hails from the Power House which stood on Washington Road.

Richard lived there between 1952-87. The house was owned by the North Eastern Electricity Board. He was one of the first pupils at Hylton Red House Comprehensive when it was opened in 1964 and was often 'chased' when playing football on the green by Sheriff Stan Reid (see page 17).

Richard joined Sunderland County Borough Fire Brigade in 1970 serving at Fulwell Fire Station. He moved into Tyne and Wear Brigade on the creation of the Metropolitan County in 1974 and he has been able to make it to the 'top' of his profession in his own County.

Richard *(right)* and brother Les in the garden of the Power House in 1971. Les was a Detective Constable in the Northumbria Police when he died on duty in 1991.

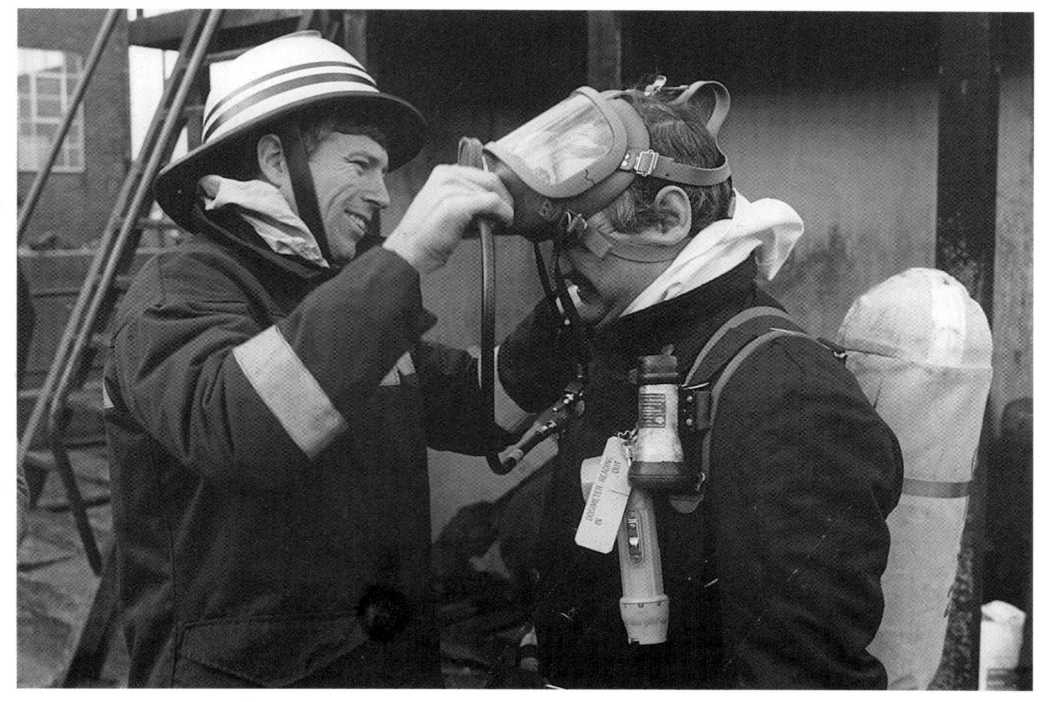

Fire Chief Richard Bull helps out a fireman in breathing apparatus

THE AERODROME

Sunderland Airport in the early 1980s.

Early Days

The first airfield at Hylton was established during the First World War. B-Flight of No 36 Squadron of the Royal Flying Corps arrived in October 1916. In August of the following year A-Flight took over and helped defend the Sunderland area against Zeppelin raids.

Only three days after the Armistice two RAF men died in an explosion and fire at the Aerodrome. The men had been using petrol to clean their clothes when the vapour was ignited by a boiler fire next door.

After the war the airfield reverted back to farmland.

On St Patrick's Day 1930, 607 (County Durham) Squadron Auxiliary Air Force was formed. Thus when war did come the RAF were not as unprepared as perhaps other services.

Below: Hawker Demons from 607 Squadron over Sunderland. This two-seat biplane was based at Usworth from 1936 onwards. By 1940, 607 Squadron had an aircraft that was a real match for the enemy - the Hurricane.

The Gold Rush

After the First World War the huts built at Hylton Aerodrome were abandoned. The Liberty Villas stood empty when many young families in neighbouring Usworth and Washington had no home of their own. On 31st March 1921 some of these people decided to seize the huts. They staked out their claim by writing their names on the doors and placing one piece of furniture in the hut. Two buildings with large ovens that were used to cater for the servicemen were the first to be snapped up.

Within days there were 38 families, comprising around 150 men, women and children, on the site. Usworth Co-op sent their reps to take orders and one man set up his own shop there.

As the heads of the families were ex-servicemen themselves their claim to the disused airmen's huts was seen as justified.

Blackadder Goes Forth

In the early days of World War Two 607 Squadron was with the British Expeditionary Force in France. Flight-Lieutenant Francis Blackadder was one of those who distinguished himself doing reconnaissance work and accounting for three enemy aircraft. After Dunkirk 607 Squadron arrived back at Usworth just in time for the Battle of Britain.

On 13th August 1940 Herman Goerring launched *Adler Tag* (Eagle Day) which was planned to give the Luftwaffe air superiority over Britain within four days. Two days later the Norway-based *Luftflotte* (Air Fleet) launched a massive raid on the North East. A hundred Heinkel bombers and Messerschmitt fighters attacked RAF airfields and industrial targets in the region. A dozen Hurricanes from 607 Squadron were led into battle by Blackadder. This was to prove the Usworth men's finest hour as they downed eight Heinkels.

Before Blackadder became a flying ace he had excelled at Rugby Union. He had helped Scotland win the international championship in 1938 and was in the side that beat England at Twickenham.

From Far and Wide

During the last war a large contingent of airman stationed at RAF Usworth were from overseas. For a time New Zealander N.J. Mowat was the Squadron's Commanding Officer. He was killed in action in early 1943.

As well as Kiwis there were Australians, Canadians, Poles, French and Dutch.

Many of these men also lost their lives during the war. Of 31 Allied war graves at Castletown Cemetery 22 are from the Commonwealth and Occupied Europe.

An aerial view of Usworth Airfield around 1930.

During the last war the Three Horse Shoes was used as a Mess for Officers from RAF Usworth. The 'Shoes' stood only a stone's throw from the airfield's entrance gate. A watch tower was built on stilts on the pub's roof.

Polish Hero

The *Sunderland Echo* of 29th December 1981 recalled the heroism of a Polish airman in 1942. Martin Simpson, a first aid volunteer at Usworth during the war, told how shortly after take-off a Polish pilot radioed the Control Tower that he was experiencing problems with his aircraft.

He was flying over Station Road in Usworth and he said he would try and bring the plane down in a field rather than crash into one of the houses in the street. He could not make it to the field, but he still did everything he could to save the people in the house by crash landing in the street. I got on my bicycle and rode off, but we could not get near the plane because its bullets were flying in all directions shattering windows in the street. I shudder everytime I go past the spot on the bus and I have done everything I can to try and trace the pilot's family to tell them of his bravery.

Above: Castletown Cemetery is the final resting place for over thirty Allied flyers killed in the last war. A few yards away are the graves of ten German servicemen *(below)*.

The Day A Flying Fortress Dropped In

Jim Weatherill remembers:

As a youth I was a member of 373 Squadron Air Training Corps, based at Bede Towers, Burdon Road, Sunderland. On Sunday afternoon, 11th November, 1943 we were at Usworth Aerodrome, I think at this time it was a base for Hurricanes. We used to do fatigues and odd jobs. In return we received instruction in various subjects, including aspects of safety, packing parachutes, and how to operate them in emergency.

At times we also received flights in Avro Ansons or De Haviland Rapides from anything from 10 minutes to 35 minutes. On this particular day we had had flights in a De Haviland Rapide for some 15 minutes. It is difficult to remember the exact time, but it was daylight around 4 pm, when we heard, then saw a B17 Flying Fortress circling the airfield. It circled two or three times with what I think was engine trouble or possibly low on fuel.

It made a pass over the field then made a good landing. Although there were tarmacadam runways they were short and the plane came to a rest on a grassed part of the field. With great excitement we dashed forward as the crew disembarked, 10 or 12 crew members in all.

Air Cadet Jim Weatherill

I distinctly remember the sight of one of the rear gunners throwing 5 inch ammunition to us for souvenirs, and some time later their visit to our Squadron at Bede Towers.

The Flying Fortress

There were hundreds of B-17s based in Britain during the war. While the RAF made night raids on Germany the Americans attacked during the day. To defend themselves during these dangerous daylight raids planes like the Flying Fortress had as many as 13 machine guns in the nose, chin, tail, dorsal, ventral and even the radio compartment. The bullets young Jim Weatherill and his friends were thrown in 1943 came from one of these gun turrets.

Airshows

Before the Aerodrome closed the Airshow was a popular annual event.

Sunderland Air Day on Sunday 14th June 1981 attracted an estimated 50,000 people to the airfield and surrounding hills.

Roar of the Jets

When the Airshows were held in the 1960s and '70s we used to have jets doing low level flyovers. If we were inside our house on Town End Farm when a jet went over you thought the roof was going to be knocked off.

Stuart Bell

Above: A local youngster gets a close up view of a light aircraft at the airfield.

Below: One of the most popular aircraft on view was a US Air Force Hercules.

Above: A Supermarine Spitfire - the most famous RAF aircraft of World War Two.

Right: An American Sikorsky helicopter.

Below: Crowds on the airfield.

Parachute Club

In the 1980s 700 people a year made their first parachute jump at Sunderland Airport. After a full day's training they boarded a light aircraft and then made their jumps under the close supervision of an instructor.

A parachutist jumping from a plane at Sunderland Airport. Sadly not all jumps ended safely.

Touchdown in front of the Three Horse Shoes in 1978.

Two parachutists descending together seen from Ferryboat Lane playing fields.

Sad Sight

I was walking along a path in front of Castle View School one Saturday evening in the 1980s when I noticed parachutists in the distance. A number of my friends had recently taken their first jumps so I followed the descents with interest. I saw one plummet earthwards without the chute opening. The landing was obscured by the houses of Hylton Castle. When I got home to Town End Farm, one of the friends who had recently made his first parachute jump, called round. When I explained what I had seen he said it would have just been a streamer to show the wind direction. On the Monday morning the front page of the *Daily Mirror* had the story of a young woman skydiver who had been killed at Sunderland when her chute failed to open.

Mark Taylor

Right: Built between the wars, the Lamallar hangar is the only part of the old aerodrome to survive as part of the Nissan plant. This building was said to have been haunted by the ghost of a Canadian pilot who died when his Hurricane crashed.

In 1962 Sunderland Corporation bought Usworth Airfield for £27,000 and renamed it Sunderland Airport. The following year Sunderland Flying Club was formed. A Parachute Club and Gliding Club followed.

Little & Large

A light aircraft flies over a Vulcan bomber at Sunderland Airport. The Vulcan was the largest plane to land at the airfield and is now one of the prize exhibits at the North East Aircraft Museum.

This 'Delta wing' aircraft was designed specifically to carry Britain's Atomic bombs. From the 1950s until the '80s the Vulcan was an integral part of this country's nuclear deterrent. In 1982 the Vulcan was used to bomb Stanley Airfield in the Falklands War.

Nissan

The Nissan car factory was officially opened by Prime Minister Margaret Thatcher on 8th September 1986. The £50 million plant on a 297 acre site employed 470 workers at that time.

The workforce soon rose and Bluebirds were rolling off the Nissan production line at the rate of one every four minutes.

There are still a number of popular myths surrounding Nissan. The car giant points out that there are no exercise programmes before the start of each shift and there are no company songs or slogans. In fact they appear more egalitarian then most firms in the region. All employees work under the same terms and conditions of employment, there are single status subsidised canteens and there is no privileged parking.

The massive Nissan plant was built on the site of Sunderland (Usworth) Airport. The only part of the aerodrome that remains is the aircraft hanger. The Aircraft Museum is situated across the road to Nissan's main entrance.

Below: Nissan workers hail the award-winning Micra.

TOWN END FARM

A glider soars over Town End Farm.

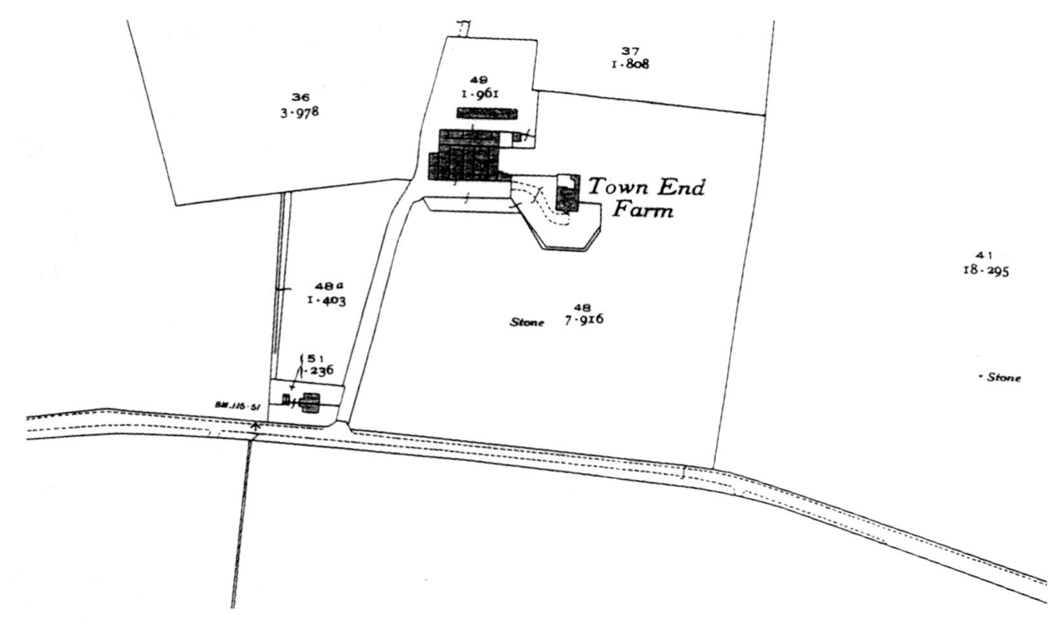

A map from just before the last war showing Town End Farm and surrounding fields.

The Final Frontier

When Sunderland's post-war housing development claimed the 150 acres of Hylton Castle Farm the owner of the farm Richard 'Dixie' Thompson thought 'never again'. When he took over Town End Farm he was assured this farm would be safe from developers. He was devastated to learn less than five years later he was to lose this farm as well. He fought a compulsory purchase order at a public enquiry held at the Town Hall. He cited record harvests of wheat and one of the highest milk productions in the county as reasons he should be allowed to keep his farmland. This was to no avail as the Secretary of State confirmed a new housing estate would be built on the land - the present day Town End Farm.

Right: The old farmhouse has survived in the modern Town End Farm estate.

Old Hand

When the Council acquired Town End Farm for the new housing estate one of the farm's workers decided to call it a day. Eighty-year-old Jack Pollard had worked on farms since he was 13. At the turn of the century he learned thatching and farm stacking which kept him in work for the next sixty years. When he began stacking he earned 18 shillings a week. At this time a shilling bought four ounces of tobacco, two clay pipes and two pipe covers. A pint of beer cost only 2½d. Shortly after Town End Farm was sold Jack came out of retirement to teach his skills to youngsters.

The Farm

When Town End Farm went up for auction in 1750 Jacob Yellowley still had four years to run on his tenancy. He paid £80 per year for the farm, this included a house, stable, barn, byre and hemble (cow shed). All the buildings were built of stone and were covered with pantyles.

Lady Farmer

In the middle of the last century widow Anne Spraggon worked Town End Farm with her sons and daughters. She also employed five labourers on the farm of over 200 acres.

Town End Farm

By the mid-1960s Town End Farm Estate was complete with a total of 2,342 houses and flats. The estate's population stood at 8,190 with an average of 3.26 people per dwelling.

Town End Farm seen from the top of Downhill in 1997. The Nissan plant is in the distance with Penshaw Monument on the left of picture.

Way Out West

When we moved to Town End Farm in the summer of 1965, I could not believe our new house. Having lived down Hendon it was a complete surprise to find such a modern home. Although our house near the bus terminus must have been up for five years, to us it was 'brand new.' Out of the back there was the hill and quarries. Our name for the hill was the 'Ponder' shortened from Ponderosa. No doubt to the first residents of the estate the large expanse of land appeared like the ranchland of TV's *Bonanza*.

David Clarke

Soon Dated

Even though Town End Farm was a showpiece of modern housing some of its design features were soon dated. One of these was the cold storage larder in the kitchen. This was situated next to the back door. It had a concrete shelf and had a grill in the wall to allow for ventilation. Soon after these were constructed, refrigerators became an everyday item in homes making the larders obsolete.

Victoria Smith

Ponder Sledge Ride

In wintertime after a fall of snow we used to sledge down the Ponderosa. I remember one time coming right from the top head-first lying flat on my stomach. Right at the bottom I was heading straight for a lamp post. Instead of jumping clear I stayed on and hit the lamp post with a shudder. One of my friends said the light went off after the collision. Luckily I only glanced the concrete post with my shoulder.

Tony Martin

Blackwood Road in the 1980s with the 'Ponder' in the background. Before Nissan was built the hill used to be packed with people during the annual airshows in summertime. While in winter the hill provided a neck-breaking sledge ride.

The idea for a workmen's club at Town End Farm dates from 1961. In that year five men went around the estate door to door to find out if there was a demand for a club. The result was that work began on building in August 1962 and was complete after only three months. By March 1963 the club in Bexhill Road had 850 members. One of the unusual services the club provided in the early days was a hair cut. As there was no hairdresser's on the estate in the early '60s they arranged for a barber to visit the club on Mondays and Wednesdays. *Below:* Committeeman Billy Farquhar outside Town End Farm Workmen's Club in 1979.

Bexhill School

Bexhill Juniors opened on 11th January 1965 with 246 children behind their desks on the first day. The Infant School was slightly behind schedule and opened a few weeks later.

When built in the mid '60s the hall of Bexhill School was a distinctive addition to the Town End Farm skyline.

Bexhill Juniors football team of 1970. Back row, left to right: Mr Lilliendale (teacher), Colin Anderson, Leslie Smith, Peter Mustard, Kevin Richardson, David Collier, Leslie Stoker, Mr Slawther (teacher). Front row, left to right: Colin Milligan, Alan Coulthard, Gary Stoker, Peter Dolan, Philip Ogle, Keith Stevenson. Kevin Richardson played for Sunderland Boys and was their top scorer in the 1970-71 season with 20 goals. Dennis Lilliendale's involvement in football led him to become Sunderland and District Primary Schools' Association's first chairman in 1971. Sid Slawther's father was a Special Constable who was killed in an air-raid while on duty outside Roker Park during the last war.

Champion Athlete

Right: Sheila Allen just after winning the North East Veterans' cross-country championship in February 1995. The following year the Town End Farm athlete retained this title and also became British Veteran cross-country champion.

The Houghton and Peterlee runner won her first England vest in 1995 when she was selected to run in the Veterans' international championships in Dublin. Her fifth place helped England to the silver medal.

On 8th November 1997 she made her third appearance for England in Ballymena, Northern Ireland. A brilliant third place gave her the gold medal in her category and helped England to gold in the team event.

Sheila has competed in 228 races and has won an incredible 98 of them and on a further 69 occasions she has been runner-up.

What's in a Name

For one year in the 1960s I went to Town End Junior School. I remember the headmaster, Mr Garbutt, used to get upset if anyone called the school Town End Farm. I remember the school was presented with a shield with this name inscribed. The headmaster returned it and insisted the word 'Farm' be removed. I could never understand the big fuss after all the school was on Town End Farm.

Jackie Turnbull

Different Weather

One sunny day about twenty years ago I set off from Town End Farm for a match at Roker Park. When I reached the ground it was shrouded in sea fog. After waiting around for a while with no change in conditions it was announced the game would not be played. I returned home to find Town End Farm still bathed in sunshine. It's amazing how different the weather could be less than four miles apart.

Mark Taylor

E Type Jaguar to Travelling Vans

Even when we moved up to Town End Farm in 1965 there was not a great deal of amenities. There were no pubs or churches. Many people shopped at Hylton Castle. Although there were some shops at Beeston Avenue these were a considerable distance for most of the estates' residents. The shops at Blackwood Road were just being built and one of the first of these was Simpsons the Bakers. The young owner used to park his blue E Type Jaguar outside the shop. There were also two 'travelling' vans which sold groceries which were permanently parked outside their owners' houses.

Angela Banks

When Town End Farm was built all the names of the streets began with the letter B. After the Baxter Road flats were renovated by the private sector they broke with this tradition. The blocks were renamed: Canterbury House, York House and Durham House.

The Fair

Before the A19 bypass was built in the 1970s a fair was held annually on the land west of Town End Farm. It always seemed to rain when the travelling fair set up there. This led to the site becoming a quagmire as people from the neighbouring estates piled in.

Tommy Jones

The Slipway & Schooner

Above: When this pub was built in the 1960s Sunderland still had a shipbuilding industry so it was no surprise that it was named The Slipway. Many of its patrons worked in shipyards such as Doxfords, Bartrams, JL Thompsons, Laings and Austin & Pickersgills.

The other pub at Town End Farm also had a nautical name - The Schooner. In the early 1990s it closed and the building was vandalized and then demolished.

Right: The Schooner provides the backdrop to the Charity Pram Race. Con Haley is pushed along by Albert Ellendon (affectionately known as Bam).

Boxing Brothers
Shaun & Chip O'Neill

Shaun and Michael 'Chip' O'Neill are Town End Farm's most celebrated professional boxers.

Featherweight Chip has just retired after a long and successful career. As an amateur he boxed for Young England and reached the Northern ABA finals. He met Castletown's Billy Hardy six times during his amateur days - each winning three bouts. For a long period he stopped boxing but returned to the ring as a pro when he joined Tommy Conroy's stable.

Younger than Chip by five years, Shaun is now approaching the top of the fight game. He started boxing at Hylton Castle and Town End Farm Boys' Club and then moved onto Sunderland ABC.

Like Chip he joined Tommy Conroy's East End gym. Fighting at welterweight Shaun is one of the hardest hitting boxers in the North of England.

Shaun *(left)* and Chip O'Neill.

Football Daft

From the age of 10 until 14 in the late sixties I was daft about football. Every spare moment I seemed to play football. On Sunday morning we played on Town End School field. The games were between anything up to fifteen aside - some were grown men running off the effects of a Saturday night's drinking. After three or four hours we would go home for dinner then out again playing in the streets. In our back street (Bletchley Avenue) we played 'gates'. Every player had a gate/goal to defend. While everyone tried to score in the other's gate. Three goals conceded resulted in you dropping out and the winner was the last one left in. If we were chased by neighbours we moved on to Baxter Road to play 'lamps'. One massive lamppost was the goal and everyone tried to score by hitting it. The game was often interrupted because it was played on a busy road.

Jimmy Allen

Clive Mendonca

Bexhill Juniors' most famous footballing old boy is Clive Mendonca *(above)*. The free-scoring striker has played for Sheffield United, Doncaster Rovers, Rotherham United, Grimsby Town and now Charlton Athletic. His recent £700,000 transfer to The Valley showed how highly Clive is rated in the football world.

Bexhill Square

Before

A block of flats at Bexhill Square in 1991 shortly prior to redevelopment.

After

Old people's bungalows that replaced the flats.

Section Four

North Hylton

A view of Hylton from the north bank of the river before the bridge was built.

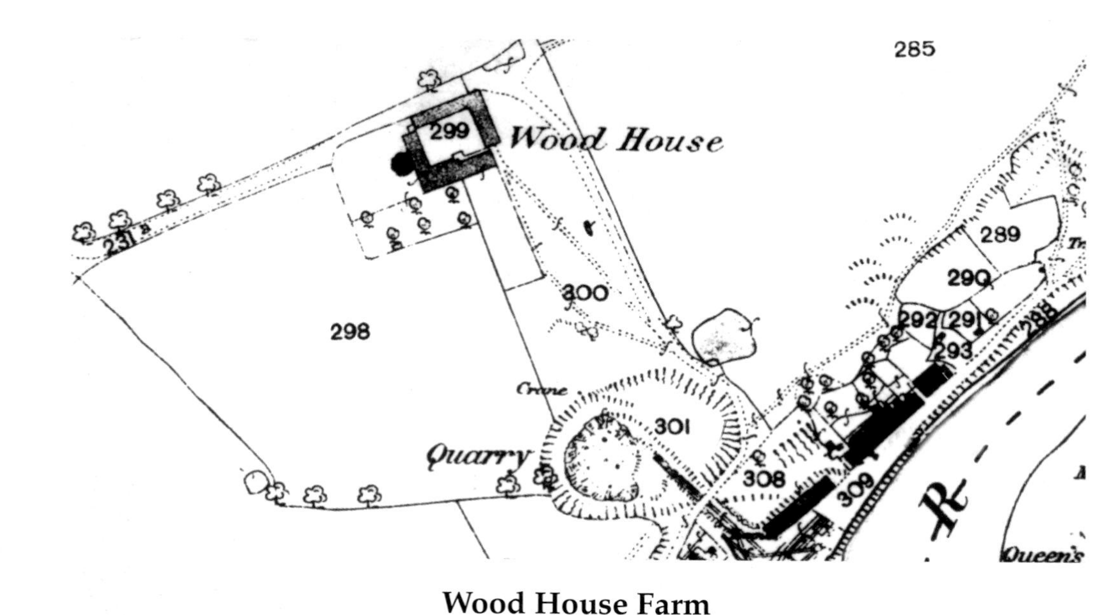

Wood House Farm

In 1750 Ann Robson was tenant at Wood House Farm at an annual rent of £115. The farm buildings included a house, stable, two barns, byre and hemble. The grounds included woods, ponds and springs.

Hylton Ferry

When James Burridge bought Wood House Farm shortly after the last war he took on more than he bargained for. He knew whoever purchased the farm and its 270 acres had to maintain the ferry link between North and South Hylton. However, after a few years problems began to emerge.

The job of ferryman was not especially appealing. There was no shelter on either bank from biting winds, hail, rain and snow. There was also a problem of people taking the boat themselves when the ferryman was having his dinner. He would often return to find the boat on the opposite bank or in mid-stream.

In the winter of 1956 Charles Darby the former ferryman refused to leave the riverside cottage that went with the job. He would not go until he had been rehoused. His replacement Charles Clarke gave in his notice and this was the final straw for the farmer James Beveridge. He locked up the boat and stopped the ferry service for good in January 1957.

Later in the year the Sunderland ferry down river ceased to operate while the previous year the ferry upriver between Barmston and Coxgreen had stopped.

Robert Surtees' *The History and Antiquities of the County Palatine of Durham* records an early reference to Hylton Ferry:

... in 1322, Robert, Baron of Hilton, granted to his Chaplain William de Hilton, the *Passage of Bovisferry* (Ox ferry where cattle were transported). The same Chaplain William shall provide a proper boat for the ferry.

The ferry for carrying horse-drawn vehicles at Hylton early this century. At this time industry lined both sides of the river at Hylton with workers travelling back and forth on the ferry.

Before its closure in 1957 the Hylton ferry only transported people across the river.

The Romans at Hylton

Roman Bridge at Hylton

In 1883-84 the Reverend Dr Hooppell put forward evidence of a Roman Bridge at Hylton. In a number of papers to the Newcastle Antiquarian Society he cited the testimony of a Mr Lister who was in charge of a shipyard at North Hylton. In the mid-1860s Mr Lister had seen tons of worked stone taken out of the river near the ferry crossing. These were taken by the River Wear Commissioners for harbour improvements. The stones were set in an oak framework along with large quantities of lead. He recalled how apprentices from the yard helped themselves to hundredweights of lead during their dinner hour. Local people called these the 'Brig Stones' and they had been in the river for as long as anyone could remember. One stone had a white metal plate clamped to it bearing the inscription:

IM — — D — — AUG.

For Dr Hooppell this dated the 'Bridge' to around 81 AD in the time of the Roman Governor of Britain Agricola.

Dam Theory

In 1983 Raymond Selkirk put forward an original theory about the stones at Hylton. Rather than a bridge he thinks the stone construction was a dam. In *The Piercebridge Formula* he puts forward the idea that Roman dams on the Wear at Hylton and Chester-le-Street would have raised the river level to allow barges to bring heavy goods to forts lying fourteen miles from the sea.

The evidence put forward by Dr Hooppell could support the Hylton Dam theory. The lack of Roman roads and the high river banks at the site lends more weight to a dam rather than a bridge at Hylton. The lead found in the remains of the structure might have been used to make the dam's joints watertight.

Early Calls for a Bridge

As early as 1817 proposals were put forward for a bridge at Hylton. The estimated cost was put at £5,000 but the scheme never got off the ground.

In February 1891 a meeting was held to consider the means by which to bring a bridge to Hylton. Architect Frank Caws unveiled a plan he had drawn up for a bridge between North and South Hylton. The owners of Hylton Castle said they would give land free on the north side of the river if the scheme went ahead. The Briggs brothers said they would also contribute £300 towards the project.

Hyltonians had to wait until the twentieth century for their bridge.

Shipbuilding

In the middle of the last century there were no less than ten shipbuilding yards at North Hylton. Ward's *Trade Directory* of 1855 lists: W. Briggs & Co, H. Carr, Hodgson & Gardners, Matthew Kirkley, J. Lister, R. Reay, T. Seymour, Talbot & Sykes, W. Taylor and Todd & Brown all shipbuilding at North Hylton as well as T. Lightfoot at Hylton Dene.

Reay's shipyard had been there since the 1790s. When the founder died his widow ran the business with the help of her brother William Potts who was himself a shipwright.

North Hylton's most famous shipbuilders was Osbourne, Graham and Company. It began iron shipbuilding in 1871 although from the beginning the size of vessels were limited by the narrowness of the river at Hylton. The yard built the 1,370 ton *Wye* for the Admiralty in 1873. More warship orders followed and the yard continued to build these right up to and during the First World War.

Cape Packet

The barque *Cape Packet* was launched from Reay's North Hylton shipyard on 10th July 1838. It had been built for Captain Christopher Lamb and partners for trade between the Cape of Good Hope and India.

In 1842 the *Cape Packet* was used to transport 150 convicts to Australia. The North Hylton-built barque spent its remaining days as a whaling ship working out of Sydney.

The last ship built by Osbourne & Graham was the self-trimming collier *Copsewood* in 1925. With the closure of the yard centuries of shipbuilding at North Hylton came to an end. In 1930 National Shipbuilders' Security Ltd was established to buy up redundant shipyards. The following year Osbourne & Graham was one of those bought out and their four berths were demolished.

Below: Shipbuilding at North Hylton in the last century.

Sunderland Rules

Towards the end of 1851 the owners of shipyards at North and South Hylton announced they would be adopting the same working conditions as those down river at Sunderland. This meant longer working hours, changes in working practices and the abolition of beer allowances. The Hylton men went on a strike that was to last many months. They received support from Sunderland Shipwrights' Association who gave £100 from their funds to help the Hylton strikers. Much was made at the time of the cutting of the beer allowance. But a spokesman for the strikers pointed out this was never a big sticking point. A large proportion of men were tee-total and the rest cared nothing about what was a paltry allowance anyway. In the end the strikers were forced to go back to work and by the summer of 1852 the Hylton men had accepted 'Sunderland Rules.'

Sales by Auction.

In Liquidation.
NORTH HYLTON.

MR. ARTHUR T CROW has been favoured with instructions to SELL by AUCTION, on Wednesday, 5th. May, 1875, at Mr. N. Gibbon s Yard, North Hylton,

THE SHIPBUILDING PLANT, consisting of Deals and Battens, Thwarts, Spauls, Pine Cuttings, Deck Deals, Saw Pit, Wood-built Workshops, Two Powerful Jib Cranes, each 50ft. Jib, and Greenheart Mainpieces. Oak and Fir Blocks, Grindstones, contents of Joiners' and Blacksmiths' Shops. Cramps, Treenails, Ringbolts, Chains, Dogs, a capital Wood Steamer, 50ft. in length, Round, Flat, and Square Iron ; Muntz's Metal in Bars and Bolts, and a quantity of Miscellaneous Lots. The Sale to commence at One for Half-past One to a minute.—Manor ouse, Sunderland, April 26, 1875.

Above: An advert for the sale of Gibbon's North Hylton Shipyard in the spring of 1875.

Ancient Shipbuilders

While working for the River Wear Commissioners near Hylton Ferry in 1888 Harry Watts discovered a dug out canoe. Harry was removing 'Brig' stones in the river when he came across the boat covered in mud. The canoe was dug out from the trunk of an oak tree. It is thought to date from the Bronze or Iron Age. In 1910 the RWC presented the canoe to Sunderland Museum and it is on display there today.

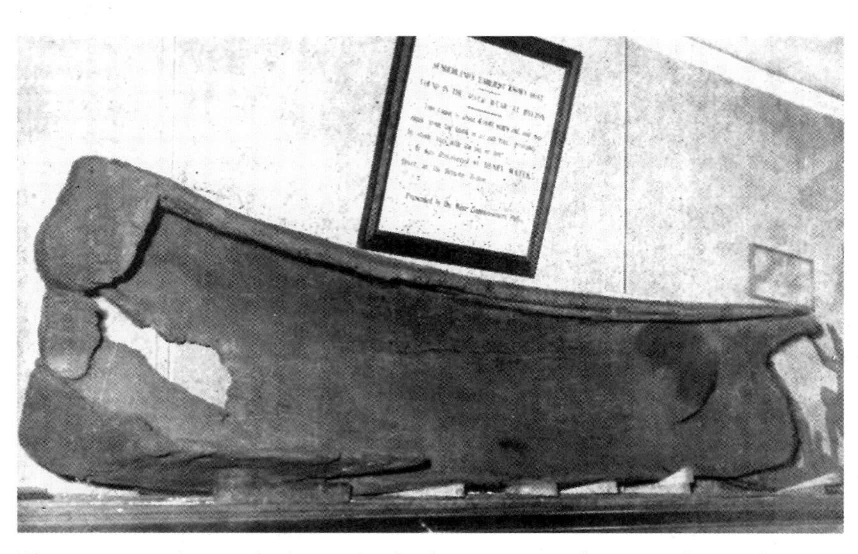

The preservation techniques in the last century destroyed any chance of later carbon dating the log boat.

Harry Watts

Harry Watts' discovery of the log boat was not the only time this famous Sunderland character made a name for himself in the area.

On 4th November 1873 Harry was talking to Squire Ettrick beside the ferry landing at North Hylton when a horse and beer dray fell off the ferry into the river. The horse valued at 100 guineas appeared doomed until Harry went to the rescue. He jumped in the fast flowing current and threw off the barrels of ale and undid the harness from the dray. Despite never having handled a horse in his life he managed to steer it to dry land.

The Squire greatly appreciated Harry's actions and gave him a £5 reward. The discarded barrels were washed ashore and Hyltonians enjoyed a night of free beer.

Above: Harry Watts proudly wears the medals he was awarded by various humanitarian societies. In his lifetime he saved the lives of 36 people, the last in May 1892 when he was 65-years-old. The famous Scottish-born American steel magnate and philanthropist Andrew Carnegie described Harry Watts as the bravest man he had ever met.

Left: An illustration of Harry Watts' horse-saving exploits at North Hylton from Alfred Spencer's *Life of Harry Watts.*

Industry at North Hylton

California Dreaming

To see North Hylton today it is hard to imagine the area was a hive of activity. Apart from the large industries like shipbuilding, steelmaking, pottery and cement works, in the past a wide variety of smaller businesses and trades flourished on the banks of the Wear at Hylton.

In the middle of the last century, there were still opportunities to be had there. The *Sunderland Herald* of 15th February 1850 reported:

It may not be amiss to request some of the go-a-head gentry of Sunderland to cast a Californian look to the hidden and comparatively undeveloped resources at Hylton.

The reference to California related to the gold rush that had taken place there the previous year.

Iron Ore

Iron Ore was once quarried on a number of sites owned by local shipbuilders. These included Edward Potts and Robert Reay's land not far from the ferry landing. The quality of this ore was said to have been of high quality. The location of these quarries meant it was only a short journey to the riverside for transport down river.

Charcoal

One of the spin-off industries of wood shipbuilding at North Hylton was charcoal manufacture and burning. The waste cuts from the yards were bought cheaply and burnt in ovens to produce charcoal. This in turn was used to produce acetic acid (vinegar). The introduction of iron and then steel not only sounded the death knell for wood shipbuilding but also for the charcoal industry.

Agriculture

The chief crops on the farms at North Hylton used to be wheat, barley, oats, potatoes and turnips. In the last century there was also stretches of ash, elm and oak in the area.

Lamp Black

There used to be a factory at North Hylton producing lamp black. This was a pigment used in making black paint. It was made from soot collected from a furnace.

Grindstones

North Hylton had quarries that yielded stones for grindstones in the 17th and 18th centuries. Grindstones and whetstones from here were exported all around the world. In 1818 (year ending 5th January 1819) over 350 chaldrons of grindstones and 4,000 whetstones were exported from the Wear. The biggest importer was North America but quantities also found their way to Scandinavia, Germany and Holland.

Sandstone

There was a quarry at Wood House at North Hylton which provided sandstone for building.

Tar

In the 1861 Census 36-year-old Joseph Mullender gave his profession as a Tar distiller at North Hylton.

Pottery

A pottery was established at North Hylton in 1762 by the Maling family. The Malings had been Huguenot refugees who settled in Scarborough before moving to Sunderland.

Rich clay beds and the riverside location for ease of transport on the Wood House estate made it an ideal site for a pottery. Hylton Pot Works started out making simple brown earthenware and later made mugs commemorating marriages and births.

The Malings claimed to have been the first in the North East to have produced printed transfers on pottery. By the end of the century the works was famous for its pink lustre ware. Other lines included: frog mugs, jugs with Masonic designs and images of the 1796 Sunderland Bridge.

Taylor Potts recalled how Mr Maling used to ride to the factory every morning on horseback crossing the river by the horse ferry boat.

In 1815 the firm transferred to Tyneside. Phillips, owners of the Garrison Pottery, took over the North Hylton factory. The pottery was owned by Austin and Dixon when it closed.

Boom Time

The outbreak of the Crimean War in 1854 signalled an upturn in industry at North Hylton. The old pottery building was turned into a forge and iron works. Shipbuilding yards sprang up on vacant lots on the riverside.

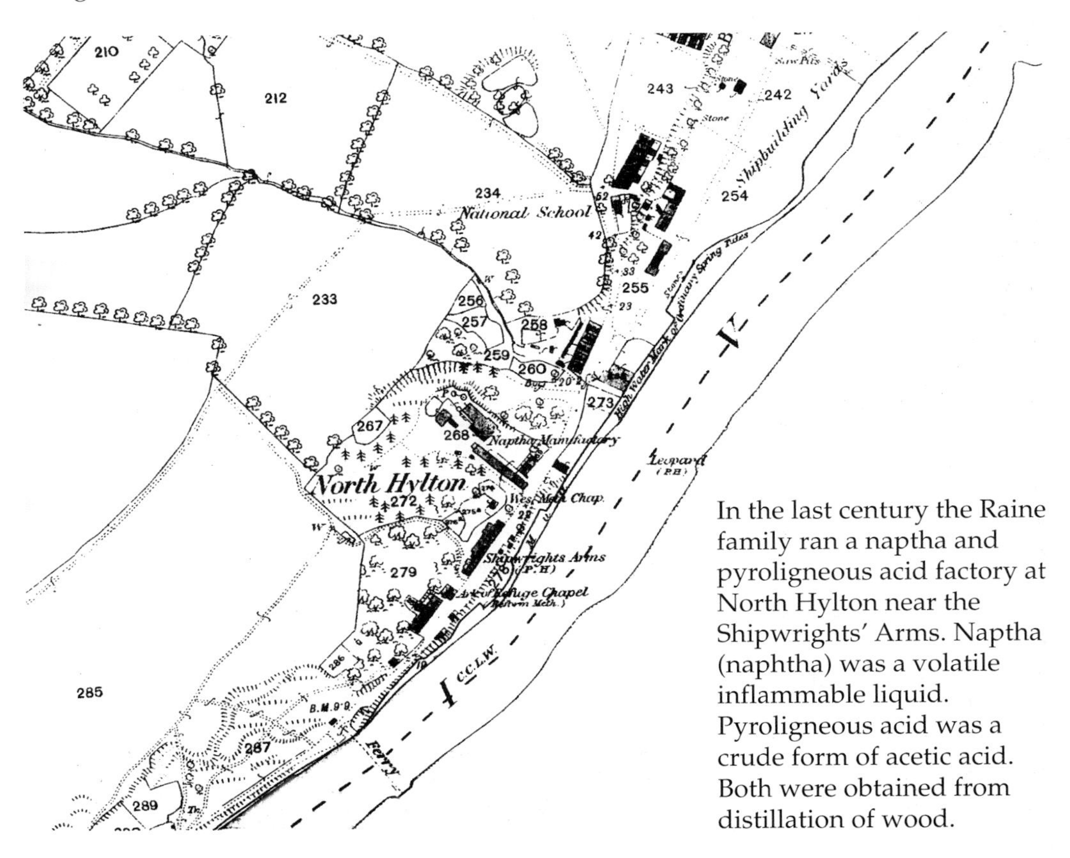

In the last century the Raine family ran a naptha and pyroligneous acid factory at North Hylton near the Shipwrights' Arms. Naptha (naphtha) was a volatile inflammable liquid. Pyroligneous acid was a crude form of acetic acid. Both were obtained from distillation of wood.

Cement Works

William Grimshaw and Sons owned a cement works at North Hylton in the last century and early years of this century.

The Grimshaws were able to persuade owners of sailing ships to return to the Wear with chalk (needed for cement making) as ballast instead of stone. This coupled with good clay deposits nearby made North Hylton an ideal location for the works.

The decline of sail ended the cheap transportation of chalk. Iron and later steel ships charged for bringing chalk from the south of England. This made cement manufactory uneconomic.

The Grimshaws were a famous Wearside family of Quakers. As well as the concrete works they had business interests in tea and coffee importing, farming, coal hauling, tallow works, carriage-making and silver-plating.

THE CEMENT WORKS NORTH HYLTON,
NEAR SUNDERLAND.

DISMANTLEMENT SALE.

A. T. AND E. A. CROW

Have received instructions from Charles Grimshaw, Esq.,
TO SELL BY AUCTION,
On FRIDAY, 23rd APRIL, 1915,
The VALUABLE PLANT AND MACHINERY,
viz.:—
Nearly New 85 h.p. Gas Engine by Field and Platt), Excellent 2-Ton Steam Derrick Crane. About 10-Ton W.I. and C.I. Scrap, W.I. and C.I. Pipes and Sundry Lots. Large Wooden Shed.
SALE AT 2 O'CLOCK PRECISELY.
Auctioneers' Office: Manor House, Sunderland.
Telephone 781.

Above: An advert for the sale of the Cement Works in 1914.

Below: The site of Grimshaw's Cement Works at North Hylton.

Danube on Wear

The Sunderland-owned brig *Danube* overturned at North Hylton on Saturday 23rd April 1898. The vessel had landed a cargo of chalk at the Hylton Cement Works and was tied up nearby. At 7 o'clock in the evening the passenger steamer *Truro Belle* was returning from a trip up river at Biddick. As the river was narrow at this point the *Danube* was moved to allow the *Truro Belle* to pass. As this was taking place the ebb tide made the *Danube* keel over.

Attempts were made to refloat her with the help of a steam crane but this failed. Masts and rigging were removed from her to allow movement for other vessels in the river.

Tragic Aftermath

A far greater tragedy occurred two days after this accident. The stranded *Danube* attracted swarms of local children. Ten-year-old Martha Adamson fell into the river from a coble alongside the vessel.

A young man dived in the river and made a brave attempt to save the girl but failed.

At the inquest held in the Victoria Hotel, Church Street at South Hylton the coroner returned a verdict of 'accidentally drowned' on young Martha.

The *Danube* stranded at North Hylton. The shop of Robert Riddell, grocer and postmaster, can be seen in the background.

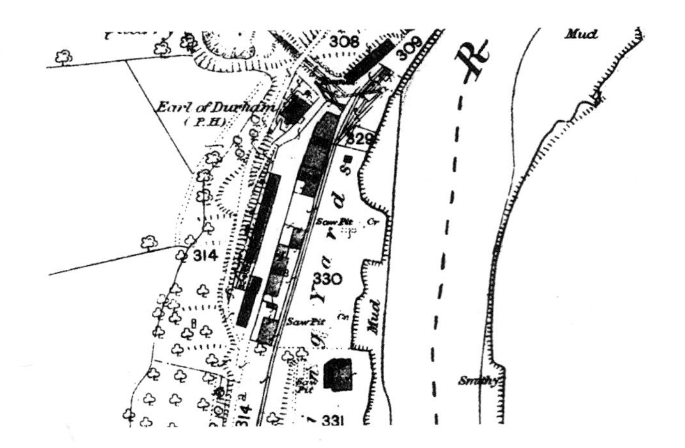

Weak Spirits

In March 1878 Elizabeth Dobson, landlady of the Earl of Durham, appeared at the Petty Sessions. She was fined five shillings and costs for selling whisky and rum adulterated with water. Superintendent Harrison had bought a pint of whisky which was 37 per cent under proof and a pint of rum which was 35 per cent under proof.

Early Aviators

Robert Welford helped by sons George and Charles built an early aeroplane at the Mansion House at North Hylton in 1910. Robert had a background in designing airships and George had worked in France in a factory building flying machines. The Welfords combined to construct a four-cylinder air-cooled engine monoplane. On 7th June George Welford got the plane off the ground but a gust of wind forced it down and damaged a wheel.

At this time Boldon Racecourse was another centre of early aviation in the district. On 1st August 1910 Madame Franck gave an exhibition of powered flight in front of a crowd of 8,000 people. Tragedy struck when the plane hit a flag pole and crash landed. A 15-year-old local boy was killed instantly but the French aviator escaped with a broken leg and cuts and bruises.

Beer Cellar

Years after The Oak Tree public house closed the building was owned by my dad. The pub's cellar had been filled in by previous owners and it was my job to dig it out. It took days of backbreaking work to get it back to how it was when beer flowed there.

Gordon Burnham

On 10th September 1892 Henry Todd, then landlord of the Shipwrights' Arms, appeared before Sunderland Magistrates on the charge of being drunk and disorderly in his own pub. Five days before, a policeman had found the landlord in a 'very drunken condition' behind the bar. He became abusive and when the constable returned two hours later he found Todd lying in a back room still drunk. The Bench fined the tippling licensee £2 and costs.

Locals still know this popular riverside pub as 'Swanies' after John Swan who was landlord from the mid-1930s.

Madman at North Hylton

The peace and tranquillity of North Hylton was shattered on 28th June 1927 with the murder of local 'bobby' Mattie Straughan. That evening PC Straughan went to Liberty Villas to serve a summons on Edward Lloyd for stealing pipes from huts that were being demolished near his home. These buildings near the Three Horse Shoes pub were constructed by the military for the airfield during the war.

Thirty one-year-old Lloyd, who was unemployed at the time, in a moment of madness blasted the constable with his shot gun. He then finished him off with a second round. The officer from West View in Castletown left a widow and three children.

At his trial at Durham Assizes Lloyd pleaded insanity. During his first appearance in the dock he wept throughout like a child. The court heard how while serving in France in 1916 Lloyd had been injured in an explosion. Thereafter he suffered mental illness.

The jury found him guilty but with a strong recommendation for mercy. Although the judge was forced to pass the death sentence, the Court of Appeal commuted this to detention as a criminal lunatic for life.

The Steady Decline

The population of North Hylton in 1901 stood at 1,715. As the century has progressed there has been a steady decline. By 1948 the population was down to just over one hundred people living in 20 cottages. The community was served by two pubs and a post office. The closure of the ferry in 1957 dealt the village a further body blow. To get to South Hylton now entailed a long journey down to Alexandra Bridge and back up the opposite riverbank. Houses continued to be demolished with no new ones being built. People were forced to move to areas such as Castletown. Although a bridge was finally built in the 1970s North Hylton today is just a shadow of what it once was.

One of the few surviving houses at North Hylton. At one time this was a bustling community.

CASTLETOWN

A postcard with a Castletown scene sent to Mr A. Lily of 7 East View in the village on 16th May 1906.

Wear Rolling Mills

It took only six months from the time the foundation stone was laid until the Wear Rolling Mills opened on 2nd November 1870. The owner was shipbuilder Thomas Oswald, who no doubt supplied his own yards with the works' finished product. The works consisted of 120 puddling furnaces, 2 puddling mills, 3 bar mills, 6 steam hammers, fitting, smiths and joiners shops. The 21 acre site needed a large supply of water and so a reservoir was formed nearby.

A view of Wear Rolling Mills from across the river. In the distance far left is The Castletown (now Crown and Anchor) public house.

Origins of Castletown

When the Wear Rolling Mills were built at Hylton Dene in 1870 the owner also erected houses for his workers. He appointed architect John Tillman and local building firms to construct these houses. Architect John Tillman is most famous for designing Sunderland Museum and Art Gallery in Borough Road in 1879.

The first houses to be built were named Oswald Terrace. A look at the 1871 Census reveals the occupants of this street. At Number 1 was the Manager of 'Hylton Iron Works', Edward Hillman and family. Like many others in the terrace he had moved from Hartlepool to work and live in Castletown. Other workers had moved from Consett, Jarrow, Darlington and farther afield.

Numbers 2 - 18 Oswald Terrace housed a variety of trades from the Works such as Millwrights, Blacksmiths, Furnacemen and Ironworkers. The birthplaces of these workers were also widespread: Staffordshire, Yorkshire, Monmouthshire and Worcestershire. Numbers 19 - 24 Oswald Terrace were still being built at the time of the 1871 Census.

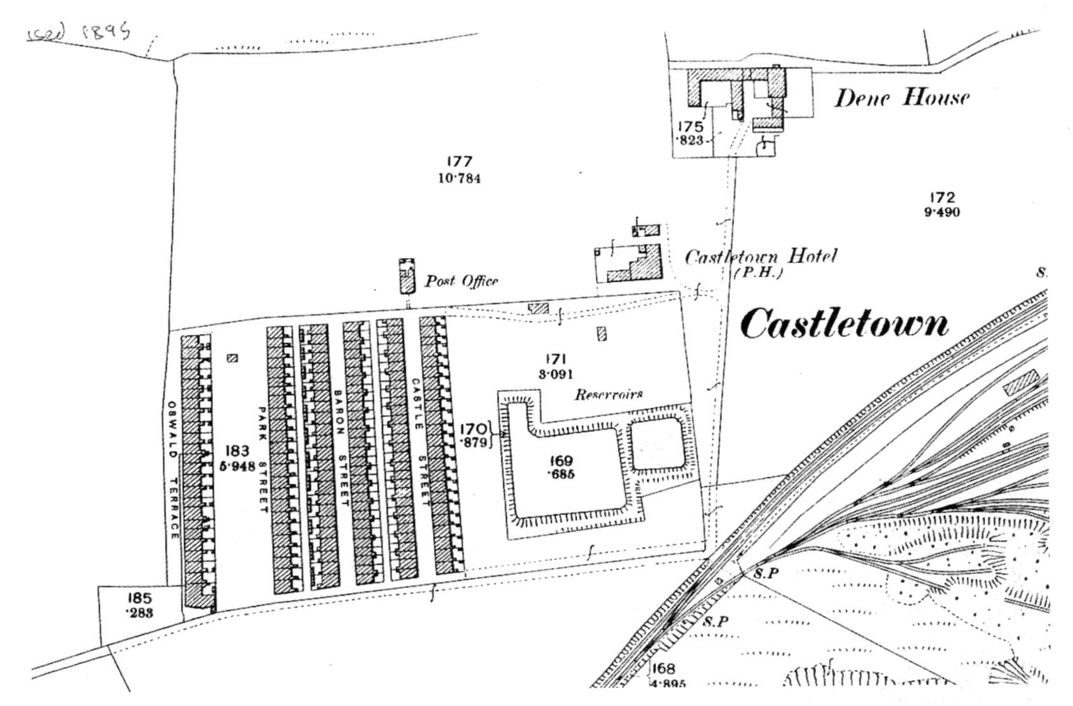

An Ordnance Survey map from the last century showing the first streets in Castletown: Oswald Terrace, Park Terrace, Baron Street and Castle Street (known by locals as Monkey Road). The latter got its unusual name from the high wooden steps at the rear of the houses which the occupants had to climb up like monkeys. A wooden butcher's shop on wheels stood at one end of Park Terrace while a similar structure at the other end sold groceries.

Castletown Remembered

In the 1950s Mansfield Gibson recalled his childhood in the early days of Castletown.

My grandfather, Percy Gibson, of Darlington, took over the management of Castletown Steel Works, my father and his brother being given charge of the Rolling Mills. Castletown was little developed in those days and I well remember the wooden butcher's shop on wheels and the wooden chapel.

I have also a dim memory of a certain R.C. priest, Father Turnerelli, coming to our house periodically to receive donations, voluntarily deducted from the wages of the many Irish workmen in support of their Catholic connexions.

New Wave

The owners of the Rolling Mills at Castletown got into difficulties and went into liquidation. The Works later reopened bringing in a fresh wave of people to the village. The *Sunderland Daily Echo* of 2nd June 1888 reported:

Some labourers have just been started at the Castletown Rolling Mills, where there is a good deal of labouring work to be done before any work can be carried on. During the past day or two several puddlers and others from Middlesbrough and Consett have been making enquiries about houses. They have been drawn here by the announcement of the works having been bought by an enterprising firm of iron manufacturers.

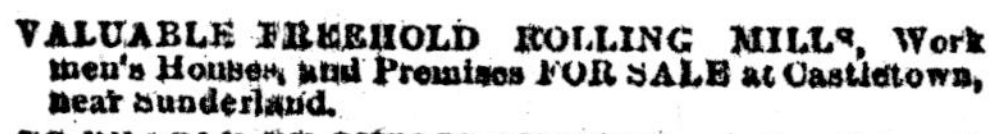

VALUABLE FREEHOLD ROLLING MILLS, Workmen's Houses, and Premises FOR SALE at Castletown, near Sunderland.

TO BE SOLD BY PUBLIC AUCTION, at the QUEEN'S HOTEL, Sunderland, on Thursday, 12TH JANUARY, 1888, at 2 p.m. prompt.

MR GEORGE BARNES, AUCTIONEER, all that VALUABLE FREEHOLD WORKS AND PROPERTY, situate on the North Bank of the River Wear, at Castletown, near the Port of Sunderland, in the County of Durham, comprising an area of about 36 acres, together with the IRON WORKS AND ROLLING MILLS, Engines, Boilers, Machinery, and Premises therein, and which is known by the name of THE WEAR ROLLING MILLS, together with a quantity of loose Stock, Stores, Tools, Waggons, and Locomotive Engines, &c.; and together also with

175

FIRST-CLASS WORKMEN'S DWELLINGS AND ONE MANAGER'S HOUSE. Further information and copies of Particulars and Conditions of Sale, with Plan of Works, may be obtained on application to Mr W. D Pratt, South Hylton; or to

MR ROBERT THOMAS WILKINSON,
53, West Sunniside, Sunderland; or to
MESSRS KIDSON, MCKENZIES, AND KIDSON,
Solicitors, John-street, Sunderland.

The works may be inspected at any time on application to Mr John [illegible], the Manager at the Works, Castletown, Sunderland.

Above: An advert for the auction of the Rolling Mills and Iron Works from January 1888.

Above: These houses in Castle Street were built after those that went up in 1870 as was Barron Street *(below)*.

Bird Cage

In the 1960s Oswald Terrace and the other original streets were demolished to make way for modern housing. The 'Bird Cage' or 'Aviary' now stands on the site. All the groves and roads are named after birds: Robin, Linnet, Wren, Thrush and Chaffinch.

Oswald's Town

The village of Castletown appears to have come in to existence by the efforts of one man - Thomas Oswald. Therefore, it could well have been named after him. It might have been called Oswaldtown, Oswaldville or as it was built on the Hylton estate - Hylton Oswald.

Hylton Colliery

Wearmouth Coal Company bought the Wear Steel Works, 36 acres of land and 190 workmen's cottages for £37,000. The company began work on sinking the first shaft in March 1897.

In October 1900 the mine was still being developed but was still producing 500 tons of coal a day. Output almost doubled when Hylton was at its peak and the workforce topped the one thousand mark.

In 1907 the coal company bought the whole of the 2,000 acre Hylton Castle Estate including the castle. As they already owned the coal rights the purchase was made as an investment.

In the late 1970s Hylton was one of a number of smaller Durham collieries to close.

Members of Hylton Lodge parade with their banner. Prior to the 1960s a portrait of Keir Hardie took pride of place on the banner. This was replaced with a view of Hylton Castle on one side and the Aged Miners' Homes on the other.

Left: Hylton Colliery in the early years of this century.

The hazardous nature of the industry in the early years was reflected in the accident statistics. From 1900 up to the First World War there was an average of one fatality a year at the mine.

Right: The original Hylton Lodge banner depicting Keir Hardie can be seen in the Coal Exhibition at Sunderland Museum.

Keir Hardie

The early Labour leader was a frequent visitor to Wearside from the 1890s up to the First World War. Hardie was elected to Parliament as an Independent Socialist MP in 1892 and in the following year founded the Independent Labour Party.

On 17th April 1895 Hardie addressed a meeting at the Miners' Hall in Monkwearmouth. At the same meeting Mrs Pankhurst, the women's rights campaigner, also spoke. On his trips to Sunderland Hardie often shared the platform with one of the town's MPs Thomas Summerbell

Not all Wearsiders appreciated Hardie's visits: on one occasion he was booed by the 'posh' inhabitants of Roker Park Road.

Hylton Colliery finally closed in 1979 and work started on clearing the site for redevelopment.

CASTLETOWN WORKMEN'S CLUB.

Castletown Workmen's Club was built at a cost of £3,000 and was opened on 16th April 1910. On the ground floor there was a billiard room, bar and sitting room. The first floor comprised a games room and reading room.

Cocktail Bar in Flames But Beer Safe

A few days before Christmas 1962 a cocktail bar at Castletown Club was gutted by fire. The bar had only been opened three months before the fire struck. The total cost of the damage ran to £3,000. The fire led to the electricity supply being temporarily cut off so the committee had to meet by candlelight.

Just before the fire the club's 940 members had been given ten free pint tickets each.

Castletown Workmen's Club today. A modern extension is just one of the changes that has been made to the building in the eighty odd years since it was completed.

When the Rolling Mills were built in 1870 many of the migrant workers were Primitive Methodists. For the next 33 years the congregation worshipped at a small building in Castletown. At the beginning of 1903 they moved to a reading room owned by the Colliery Company. At the turn of the century the opening of Hylton Colliery had brought in a new wave of Primitive Methodists from the villages of Durham. At this time the Sunday School alone had over 200 scholars and there was an urgent need for a large permanent chapel. This was built at a cost of almost £1,000 and opened on 10th October 1903.

Above: An illustration of how the chapel looked at its opening in 1903.

Left: Castletown Methodist Church in Howard Road is still going strong today.

Bringing Art to the People

In May 1957 regulars of The Castletown public house *(right)* were greeted by an unusual sight - an art exhibition! Landlord William Young allowed South Shields Art Club to display their pictures in his pub. The walls of the music room were adorned with fifty paintings for a two week period.

Castletown
Hot Bed of Football

Sunderland star Mickey Gray is Castletown's most famous football son. The young winger - wing back - full back was a regular in the club's promotion campaign and Premiership season. Over the years the tiny village has produced an amazing number of professional footballers. The record of Castletown School also reads like an early Football Centre of Excellence.

Football was played in the village as early as the 1880s. Castletown were drawn to meet the might of Sunderland in a Durham Cup tie on 20th December 1884. Perhaps for some the prospect of facing the Cup-holders was too much as only eight Castletown men turned up. The tie was forfeited but a friendly went ahead with three Sunderland reserves making up a full Castletown XI. One of the founders of Sunderland AFC, John Grayston, recalled how Colonel Briggs (owner of Hylton Castle) led the Castletown team while his sister rode around the pitch on horseback cheering her brother on. The lady's support was to no avail as Castletown were thrashed 23-0. This was Sunderland's highest ever score with James Allan contributing 12 goals to the total. Despite the one-sided result the *Newcastle Daily Journal* reported 'Briggs, Nicholson (sub), and their keeper played a good game for the losers.'

Mickey Gray

Wilf Rostron

Early this century Castletown had the strongest school team on Wearside. They won the 'Sunderland School' League championship in 1911-12, 1912-13, then once during the First World War and completed a hat-trick of victories from 1919-20 to 1921-22. Castletown provided four of the Sunderland Boys team that reached the Final of the English Schools' Challenge Shield in May 1910.

In the same season centre half G.W. Thompson became Castletown's first England Schoolboy international when he played against Wales on 16th April 1910.

Tommy Glidden became another Castletown England Schoolboy cap in 1916-17. The inside forward went on to find greater fame with West Bromwich Albion. He scored over one hundred League goals for the Baggies. The highlight of his career came in 1931 when he skippered Albion to an FA Cup triumph against neighbours Birmingham.

Gilbert Glidden was also capped for his country at Schoolboy level in 1930. He joined Sunderland but never played first team football at Roker. However, he went on to play League football for Port Vale, Reading and Leyton Orient.

The Hylton Colliery side also produced a number of players who went on to the professional ranks. Harry Bell joined Middlesbrough just after the war. The wing half made 290 League appearances for the Teessiders before Darlington manager Bobby Gurney took him to Feethams.

Arthur Wright's footballing talents were recognised long before he left Castletown School. He represented both Sunderland and England Schoolboys in 1934. He went on the Roker Park ground staff when he left school and captained Hylton Colliery Juniors for two years. When he reached his 17th birthday he signed as a professional for Sunderland. In a war-interrupted career he played 270 times for the club in the League.

Castletown's Wilf Rostron made 8 appearances for England Schoolboys in the 1971-72 season. On leaving school he decided to join Arsenal and worked his way into the first team squad. It took a fee of £40,000 to bring the hard working player back to Sunderland in 1977. After a couple years at Roker he was on his travels again, first for a long spell with Watford and later with both Sheffield clubs and Brentford.

When Castletowner Tommy Glidden lifted the FA Cup at Wembley in 1931 he had plenty of local support - 325 people travelled from Sunderland Station for the game, many of them women sporting Albion colours.

Best in England

During the 1940s and '50s Hylton Colliery had one of the strongest Junior sides in the country. In 1947 they were asked to represent England in a tournament in Strasbourg. The competition included teams from Austria, Belgium, Czechoslovakia, Switzerland and hosts France. The Hylton team (or England as they were known as for these games) were at a disadvantage from the start. Unlike England where players had to be 18 at the start of the season to qualify at Youth level the age on the Continent was 20. Despite this handicap the Hylton boys won through their group games to qualify for the Final. In the Final on the Easter Monday they were beaten by the Austrian team 5-2. After the game officials from the host club Strasbourg tried to sign Hylton's centre half Tommy Cummings. Cummings turned down the chance to play in the French League and a few months later signed for Burnley.

Tommy Cummings *(left)* in action for Burnley against Arsenal.

Cummings went on to make well over four hundred League appearances for the Turf Moor club. He replaced regular centre half Allan Brown who was later to become Sunderland manager. His outstanding form brought Cummings 'B' international and Football League honours.

Hylton Colliery winger Harry Hooper made the journey south when he signed for West Ham in 1950. He became an England 'B' international and later joined Sunderland via Birmingham City.

The Upton Park-Hylton Colliery connection continued when the Hammers signed Tony Smith in 1963. Tony, brother of famous Sunderland boxer Hughie Smith, later played for Watford and Hartlepool.

Big centre forward Norman Bell was another Castletowner who slipped through the local scouting nets. In November 1973 he signed for Wolves and was an instant success.

Right: Arthur Wright of Sunderland.

Little Big Man

Billy Hardy

One of a family of 14 brothers and sisters from Castletown, Billy Hardy, fought his way to the top of professional boxing. In a sparkling career he has held British, European and Commonwealth titles at bantamweight and featherweight. Only the sport's top prize has eluded him: three times he has failed in bids for the world title.

Billy started to box at the age of ten at Hylton Castle and Town End Farm Boys' Club. Gordon Ibinson who trained Billy in his early days at the club is now his trainer.

Right: Billy with two Lonsdale Belts - each of these were gained by winning three British championship fights.

Below: Home of Champions - Hylton Castle and Town End Farm Boys' Club.

After marking his pro debut in London on 21st November 1983 with a victory Billy never looked back. He won his next eight bouts, all in the capital, which pressed his claims as a title challenger.

Right: Billy in action against Orlando Canizales at Crowtree Leisure Centre in January 1990. The American managed to hang on to his bantamweight world title by a points decision.

Above: The Cricket Club is now known as the Billy Hardy Complex. For years the social club in the grounds has been known affectionately by locals as the 'Mickey Mouse Club.'

Right: Sunderland Boys' Kirk Hardy hopes to follow his dad to the top in professional sport.

Special Deliveries

In the late 1950s Sister Martha Fox became Castletown's resident midwife. Her first delivery in the village was Sheila Kibble. Her last was on Christmas Day 1973 when she helped bring David Meek of Ashwood Grove into the world. Sister Fox had settled in Castletown after working in London, Edinburgh, York, Hartlepool and Darlington. In a lifetime of nursing she delivered over 3,000 babies.

Staff of Harwood and Jackson outside the factory at Castletown in 1990. This old Sunderland printing firm used to have a unit at Castellain Road.

Intruders Beware

For people who have been burgled and have ideas of giving the next intruder a 'hot reception' here is a cautionary tale from the last century. The *Sunderland Weekly Times* of 2nd July 1880 reported:

THE BITER BIT AT HYLTON

In the early part of this month, a mast-maker at Hylton Dene, named George Escott, thinking someone had broken into the cabin where he kept his tools, fixed a small cannon inside the cabin so that if the visit was repeated the cannon would go off, and shoot the intruder. Having to go to Sunderland shortly afterwards, and desiring to get something out of the cabin, he opened the door, forgetful of the trap he had laid, and the cannon immediately went off, the charge lodging in his legs. The injuries he received were so severe that he was unable to move, and he lay there until his cries were heard by two men in a boat on the river, who immediately procured assistance, and had him removed to Sunderland Infirmary. It was there found that both legs were riddled with holes, some of the shot having penetrated so far that they had to be removed at the back. He was in the House for about a fortnight, when he was sufficiently recovered to return home.

Hylton Dene today.

Section Six

Downhill

Downhill Club.

Where Pedestrians Are King

From its planning stage in the mid-1960s Downhill was designed to separate the pedestrian from the motor car. Many of the streets and play areas were built to exclude road traffic.

A concert party in the early 1970s put on by Downhill Parents and Teachers Association.

Pill-Box Dangers

Bordering Downhill there are large stretches of farmland, hills, a golf course and playing fields. This provided an adventure playground for us when we moved up to the area as kids in the '60s.

There used to be old wartime pill-boxes dotted all over the Ponderosa and surrounding area. I think the idea was in the event of invasion to defend the high ground to help prevent the airfield from being overrun. These pill-boxes had walls of concrete many feet thick, small windows from which machine guns could be fired. Some still had rusted metal stands for the guns.

One day we were playing in one such concrete bunker near the golf course. There was straw inside from the corn field next to it. I saw some of the straw alight and rushed out before it was blazing. Shortly afterwards a young lad died in a fire when he was trapped in a similar pill-box on the other side of Town End Farm.

Tommy Allen

Redevelopment

Killarney Avenue

Before

A block of flats in Killarney Avenue.

After

Bungalows that replaced the flats.

Kingsway Square

Downhill Primary School

Downhill Primary School at Killarney Square opened on 2nd July 1968. The £80,000 building was designed to cater for 280 pupils.

Right: Downhill Headmaster Mr Bagley and Sheila Low in the school's early years.

Downhill pupils in the early 1970s with teachers Mr Monoghan and Miss Sheila Low.

Downhill netball team in the mid-1980s.

Downhill football team in 1973-74 season.

Downhill Workmen's Club

Downhill Workmen's Club officially opened on 6th March 1968 but it had been open for business several months prior to this. The club should have opened at Christmas 1967 but a mix up over the beer licence meant the club was dry for the first few weeks.

Two of the people behind the building of the club were Ronnie Lay and Harry Whatcott. Ronnie was Downhill's first chairman and Harry the secretary. Shortly after the opening Ronnie recalled 'From young men we had talked about founding a club. Harry and I have been round the world several times as seamen, and we always kept a look-out for suitable ideas.' The best aspects of clubs across the world helped shape the plan for Downhill.

For thirty years Downhill Workmen's Club has provided entertainment for the estate's residents.

Committeemen at the opening of the club's Games Room.

A trip leaving Downhill for Old Trafford in the early '90s. As well as trips to Sunderland matches around the country Punters' Clubs are another popular club activity.

Many 'turns' on Downhill in the early years went on to find fame. Shane Fenton and The Fentones appeared at the club in April 1968. Shane changed his name to Alvin Stardust and found chart success. Frank Carson was a regular at the club before the television show *The Comedians* brought him a national audience. Some made the opposite journey - Freddie and the Dreamers appeared well after their heyday of the '60s.

Right: An advert from the winter of 1972 when power cuts disrupted the club's entertainment.

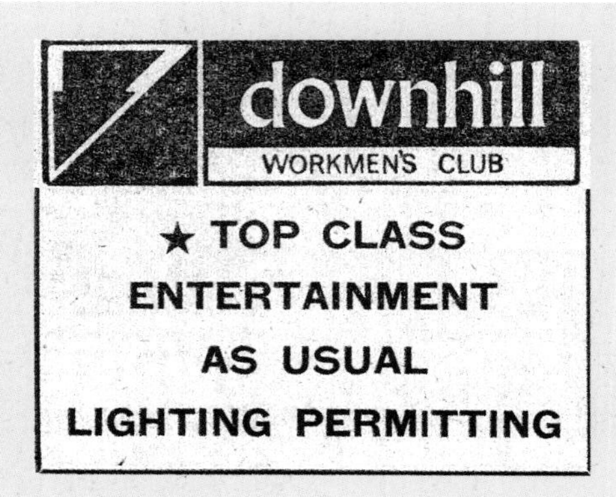

Members of Downhill Committee turning out in a football match around 1970. Back row, left to right: Billy Anderson, John Cromity, Tommy Turnbull, Mickey Henderson, Bobby Bland, Ronnie Nixon, Andy Shovlin. Front row: John Anderson (who sadly died in 1997), Bobby Stoddard, Alfie Stead, Bobby McDonald.

A Christmas Party at Downhill Club in 1981.

Civil War Battlefield

During the English Civil War there was a battle fought near Hylton Castle. The Royalist forces in the region were commanded by the Marquis of Newcastle. He faced a Scottish Army who had entered the war on the side of Parliament. At the beginning of March 1644 the Scots entered Sunderland. They were welcomed by the locals and set up camp on land between the old parishes of Sunderland and Bishopwearmouth.

On 24th March 1644 the Royalists set up camp on Boldon Hill (Downhill). The Scots left their camp at Sunderland and took up positions on the hill above Hylton Castle (Bunny Hill). They managed to get a large cannon across the Wear with the help of local keelmen. A second cannon was said to have been lost at this time. The large gun now in Barnes Park which was dredged from the river centuries later is said to be the one lost by the Scots.

The two armies clashed at around 5 o'clock in the evening. The Scots' battle cry was 'The Lord of Hosts is with us' and the Royalists shout was 'Now or Never'.

The view of the battle from the Scots' side is found in a letter sent from Whetherby a month after events:

'Upon the 24 (March), being the Lord's day, the enemy marched toward our quarters intending to have set upon us in Sermon time, and being a foggie day to have surprised us; their approach being discovered, a great part of the army was presently drawn together. The enemy sent down from Bouden (Boldon) Hill where they were drawne up, some commanded musquetiers to line the hedges betwixt them and us, and wee did the like.'

The nature of the terrain - hedges and ditches - made it difficult for either side to make a decisive attack. The fighting went on until midnight with many casualties on both sides.

'There was divers (several) killed on both sides; but the number of their slaine did verry farre exceed ours, as wee understood by the dead bodies wee found the next day upon their ground, beside the seven waggons draught of dead, and hurt men not able to walk, that the Constable of Bouden (Boldon) affirmed he saw carried away.'

Above: Alexander Leslie, Earl of Leven, Commander of the Scottish Army at Sunderland. He had learned his trade fighting for the King of Sweden, rising to the rank of Field Marshal. It was Leslie who accepted the surrender of Newcastle in October 1644.

There were further skirmishes the following day after the Royalists withdrew from their positions and retreated to Durham. The Scots almost routed the enemy's rearguard until the Royalist cavalry came to the rescue and allowed them to get away safely.

The Hylton family had the battle literally on their doorsteps with the Scots encamped on the hill overlooking the castle. Unfortunately the Hyltons backed the losing side in the Civil War. They paid a high price financially for staying loyal to the crown.

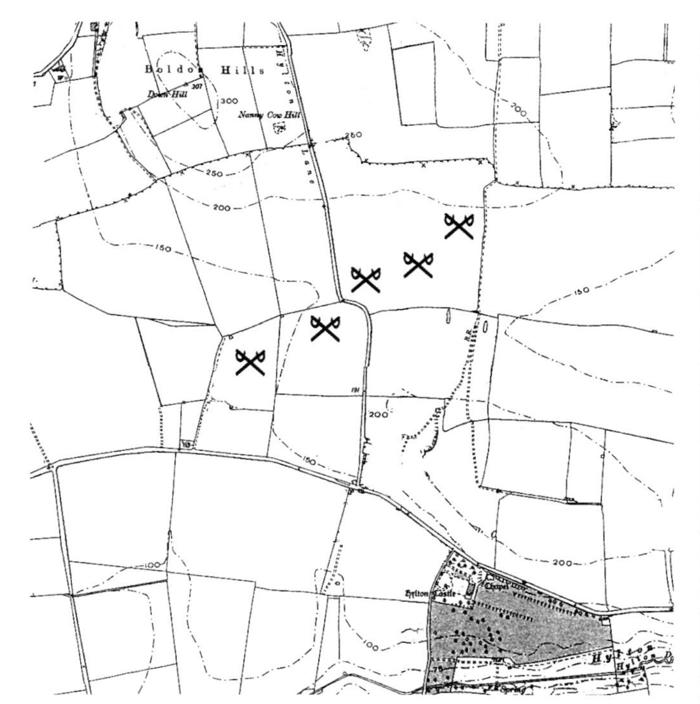

Above: A map showing the area where the opposing armies would have gathered in March 1644. The Royalists on Boldon Hills (Downhill and Nanny Cow Hill). The Scots on the hill directly above Hylton Castle.

Above: The cannon in Barnes Park the Scots were thought to have lost in 1644. It is a wonder the big gun (over 10 feet or 3m long) has survived. Crimean War cannon in Mowbray Park went for scrap to help the war effort.

Sunderland vs Newcastle

Sunderland played an important role in Parliament's victory over the Royalists in the Civil War. The city of Newcastle took the King's side and as the Tyne was the chief exporter of coal to Parliament-held London this supply ended. Sunderland stepped in and kept the capital stocked with coal from the Durham collieries. The Parliamentary forces recognised Sunderland's importance and installed a garrison in the town under Sir William Armyne.

Between 1642 and 1644 the city of Newcastle was under siege. The fall of Newcastle was described by a Scot who was there:

'Truly it was more than admirable to behold the desperate courage both of the assailants and defenders, the thundering cannons roaring from our batteries without, and theirs from the castle within; the thousands of musket balls flying at each others' faces ... the clangor and carvings of naked and unsheathed swords; the pushing of untrailed pikes, crying for blood, and the pitiful clamour of heart-fainting women imploring for mercy for their husbands, themselves and their children.'

William Lithgow

Experimental and Exact Relation upon that Famous and Renowned Siege of Newcastle (1645).

Downhill Sports Complex

Since 1993 over £2½ million has been spent on the Downhill (Community North) Sports Complex. This sum has recently been further boosted by a huge grant from the National Lottery. The award of £857,402 will go towards building a pavilion with showers and changing rooms. *Below:* An artist's impression of the planned pavilion. When fully complete the complex will have football pitches, an all-weather floodlit 5-a-side pitch, rugby pitches, netball courts, a bowling green and cricket pitch.

RED HOUSE

A toddler in the front garden of a house in Red House in 1957.

Southwick Red House Farm

In *Southwick-on-Wear Volume 4* Peter Gibson interviewed Harry and Ann Bruce who had lived and worked on both Carley Hill Farm and Southwick Red House Farm. Ann's father, James Moss, had rented Carley Hill Farm dating back to the last century. The farm had a dairy herd which supplied the local districts with fresh milk. In 1934 Ann married Harry, who had worked on the farm, and they then took over Southwick Red House Farm. The main crops were potatoes, wheat and oats. In the 1960s Southwick Red House Farm was demolished to make way for the Hepworth and Grandage factory. At this time Carley Hill Farm also disappeared as a new housing estate was built on the land.

Right: John McKenzie and Jean Bruce just before the war. The Aged Miners Homes can be seen in the background. Jean lived with her parents in Southwick Red House farm and John lived nearby.

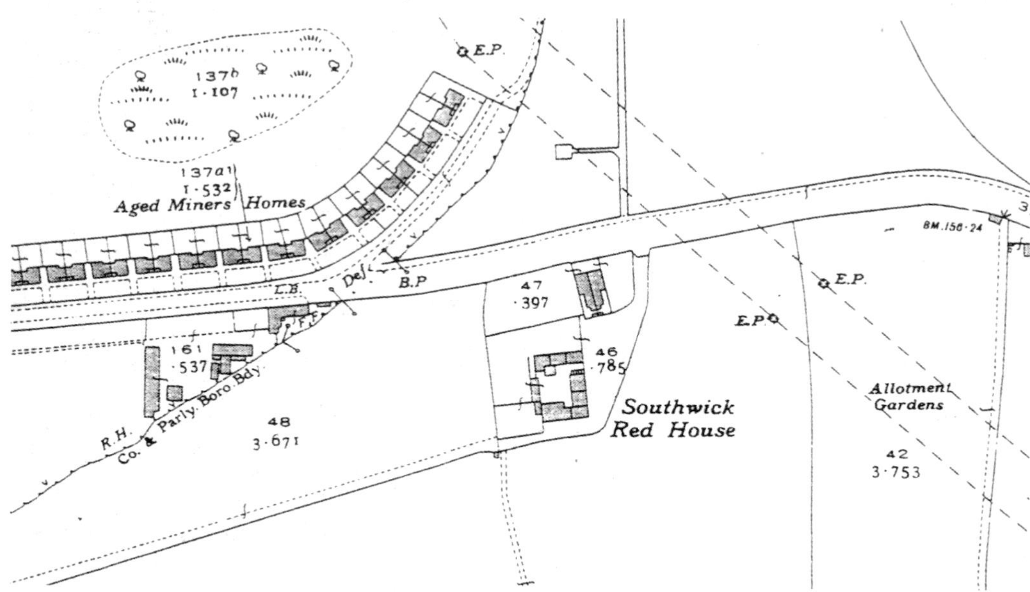

A map showing Southwick Red House Farm before the last war.

Harry and Ann Bruce with children Jean and Gordon on Southwick Red House Farm in 1940.

Jean Bruce in the old farmyard in 1948. Harry recalled the sow in picture had a litter of 14 piglets. The farm also had ducks, hens and geese.

Hylton Red House Farm

As well as Southwick Red House Farm there was a Hylton Red House Farm which stood on the site where Wear View Estate is today.

In the 1860s widower Thomas Rennoldson worked the 275 acres of Hylton Red House Farm. He employed nine men on the farm and the workload was further shared by his five sons and three daughters.

While Red House housing estate went up on much of the land surrounding the farm in the 1950s the farm itself survived until around 1970.

This was a popular name for farms around Sunderland as there were also Red House Farms at the Wheatsheaf, on Strawberry Bank and more than one at Hendon.

Age of Steam at Red House

The *Sunderland Herald* of 10th March 1871 reported a new innovation in farming:

During the present and the previous week, the tilling of the land by steam might have been seen in the large fields of the Red House Farm, on the Hylton Castle estate.

The use of steam to do the work of ploughing and grubbing though still somewhat of a novelty, has ceased to be an absolute wonder. An engine which moves itself readily backwards or forwards is placed at each end of the field, and the plough or the grubber is drawn from the one to the other ... The owners of the steam apparatus lend everything except water and coals, and the men engaged live in caravans, which are dragged from one place to another by the steam engines which travel on country roads ... improvements are profitable only in the large holdings to be found on large estates.

An illustration of a steam ploughing team similar to that which would have been employed at Red House Farm in 1871.

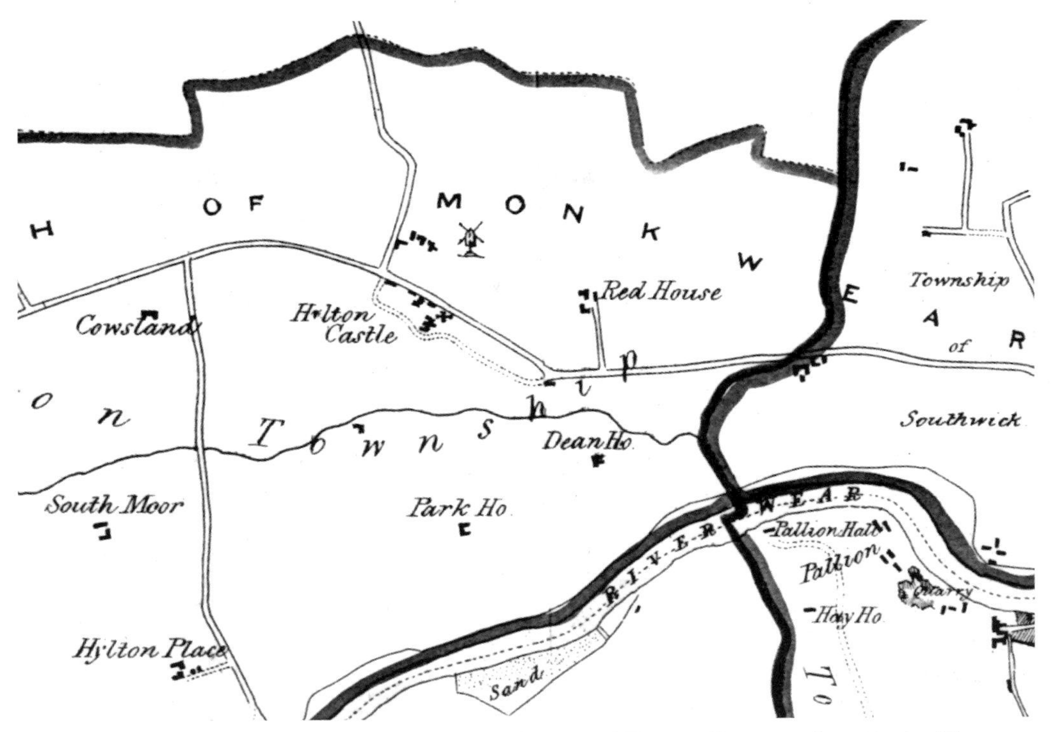

Robert Dawson's map of 1832 showing Hylton Red House Farm and a windmill on the high ground above Hylton Castle. In 1841 Peter Charlton, a miller, was living at Hylton Mill with his family.

Red House Pioneers

The first families to move on to Hylton Red House arrived in the spring of 1951. Redcar Road was the first to be occupied followed a few weeks later by Raleigh Road.

The first people to arrive at Red House came from the East End, Monkwearmouth and Southwick.

In the early years of Red House the residents had to travel to shops at Southwick for provisions. Travelling shops helped save families from some of these journeys.

By the end of the 1950s there were 2,100 houses at Red House. The 8,000 residents were served by three schools, two churches and just a few shops. The range of goods that could be bought at these shops were limited to foodstuffs. In 1957 Councillor Len Harper declared the need for a chemists at Red House. There were no pubs on the estate at this time but Red House Workmen's Club opened in 1958.

Three girls on the new Red House estate in the 1950s. Left to right: Kathleen Cairns, Annie Cairns and Catherine Ankers.

Hylton Red House Primary School

For over forty years Hylton Red House Junior and Infant School has been educating the estate's children.

Right: A class at Red House in the 1970s. The teacher Michael Davidson was a former professional footballer with Hull City. The long hairstyles shows the changes in fashion over the decades.

Left: Red House School football team in the '70s. Back row, left to right: Gary Cowell, Stuart Wilson, Anthony Buckley, Gary Mellefont, Ian Chandler, Colin Wilson, David Dodsworth. Front: Kevin Jobling, Ian Brown, Robert Thoms, Tony Nesbit, Derek Baker, Paul Judson.

Amazingly four of the team went on to become professional footballers: Chandler, Dodsworth, Jobling and Nesbit.

Mickey Horswill, one of the heroes of Sunderland's 1973 FA Cup triumph, was for a time landlord at the Shipwrights.

The Good Life

After moving to Runcorn Road from Hendon, Mrs Vera Gaffney never looked back.

In October 1959 she said Red House had its faults but they were more than outweighed by the advantages. 'The air here is wonderful. It is just like living in the country, but with the town on your doorstep.'

When families moved into new houses at Red House in the 1950s for many it was the first time they had a garden. It gave some the opportunity to build a greenhouse *(above)*.

Kitty Ankers and son Richie in the back garden of their home at Rosemary Road in the 1960s.

Continued Growth

In the summer of 1966 there were 3,399 houses at Red House and Downhill. The combined population of the two estates was 11,712. A further 392 houses were planned to be built by 1980.

Above: Rhodesia Road was named when Britain still had an Empire. Today the country the road was named after no longer exists.

Right: Red House Methodist Church in Redcar Road celebrated its fortieth anniversary in 1997.

In 1959 St Cuthbert's Church was built at Red House. Members of Holy Trinity at Southwick had raised a large part of the £25,000 building costs. The new church was dedicated by the Bishop of Durham, Dr Maurice Harland.

Bishop Harland

The Bishop returned to Red House three years later to lay the foundation stone of a school that would bear his name. Bishop Harland Church of England School cost £62,000 to build. The money came in part from the state and part from church funds.

The school was built to replace two old church schools at Southwick (St Columbia) and Bishopwearmouth which had closed.

When the Bishop officially opened the new school on 23rd April 1964 he reminded people that it was the church that had taken the lead in education a century before. It was only after the 1870 Education Act that the state stepped in and took over responsibility.

Church of England School

The first pupils to take their places at Bishop Harland School started in January 1964. These children were transferred from 14 different schools in Sunderland. All but a handful of these lived on Red House Estate.

Right: Bishop Harland netball team of 1986. Back row, left to right: Vicki Stephenson, Joanne Butler, Claire McGuinness, Michelle Shepherd. Front row: Joanne Wilson, Kelly Neale, Stella Davis.

Below: Bishop Harland nursery at Christmas 1982. Mrs Stephenson *(left)* and Mrs Horn with a class of children who will be grown up today.

Bishop Harland football team in the 1980-81 season.

Miss Whales' class of 1978-79 at Bishop Harland.

Red House Fun Run

The first Fun Run was staged on Sunday 20th June 1982 with a field of 1,283 runners. The winner was 16-year-old Ian Widdrington but he agreed to accept the schoolboy medal and let second placed Stephen Eccleston take the winner's trophy. Caroline Naisby was the first woman home and Tracy Hetherington the first schoolgirl.

The 10 mile course took runners through Town End Farm, along North Hylton Road, through Southwick, Fulwell, Carley Hill, Witherwack and back to the start.

Right: Runners in the final stretch of the 1983 race

Below: Runners in the 1984 Fun Run set out from Red House Comprehensive. Brian Rushworth set a race record when he won in a time of 51 mins 49 secs. Anne Irving won the women's race for the second successive year.

Red House Workmen's Club

Red House is one of the few workmen's clubs in Sunderland that own their club and the land it is built on. They can say proudly 'We don't owe anybody a penny'. Secretary George Semens accepts the deeds on behalf of his members *(right)*.

From Red House to Las Vegas

Many stars of show business served their stage apprenticeships in the clubs of the North. In the early '60s a young man called Jerry Dorsey appeared at Red House. The singer went on to find fame as Englebert Humperdink. Other big names include: Les Dawson, Russ Abbot, Little & Large and Bob Monkhouse.

The Victory Bar in Red House was styled on Nelson's flagship. It was opened by the Commanding Officer of HMS *Victory* in July 1967.

Members enjoy dancing at the club in May 1971. Since opening in October 1958 the club has been at the heart of the local community.

Red House Leek Club

The fame of Red House Leek Club extends far beyond the boundaries of Sunderland. Every year the prize winning leek used to be given to a famous personality. The tradition began after someone read an article about the French having no experience of the taste of the region's leeks. The club felt it was time the centre of world gastronomy should no longer be denied the delights of the leek. That year's winning leek was sent off to the Mayor of Paris accompanied by a recipe for leek soup. The Mayor replied that he had passed on the leek to his chief. Since then a host of celebrities have received the honour, these include: Brian Clough, Prince Charles, President Ford, Brendan Forster and Mike Neville.

Right: Billy Rich *(left)* and Jackie Barrass sending the winning leeks off to Prince Charles in 1971.

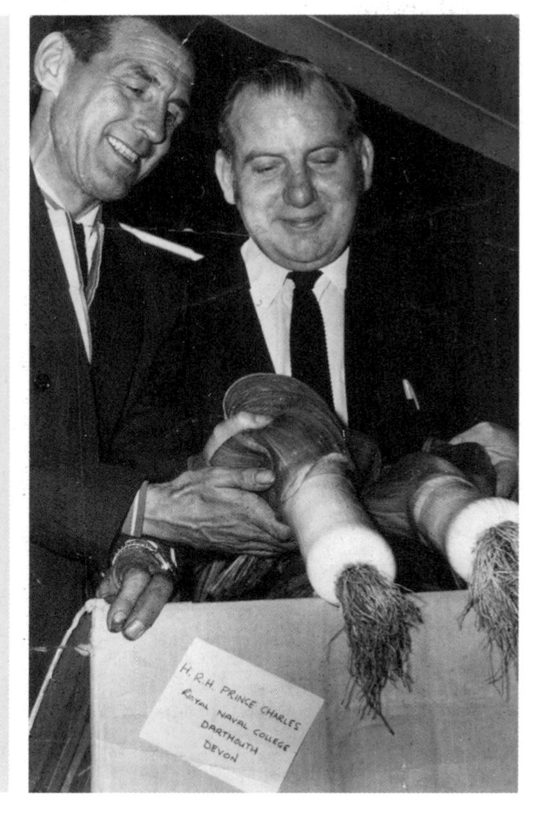

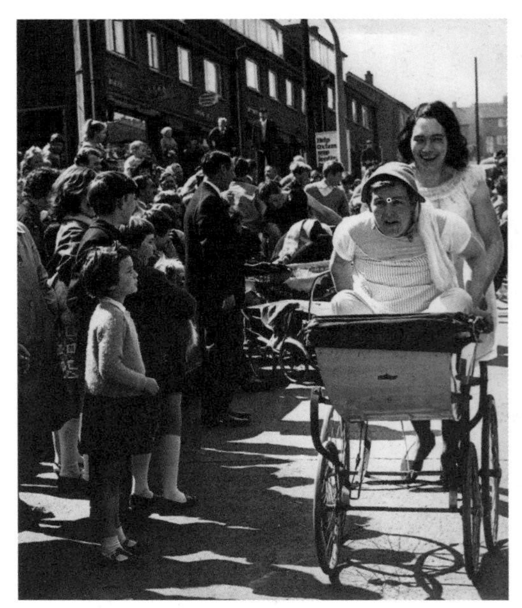

At one time the Charity Pram Race around Red House and the neighbouring estates was an annual event. After leaving the start at Red House Club the contestants called at pubs and clubs on Downhill, Town End Farm, Hylton Castle and then back to Red House. Tables full of beer were placed outside each club and pub on route. At every stop the dressed-up pram racers drank a half pint of beer .

Red House Comprehensive

Hylton Red House Comprehensive, to give its full title, was the first purpose-built comprehensive in Sunderland. These were planned to replace the old three-tier system of secondary modern, grammar and technical schools. The Local Authority gave the go ahead for the building of Red House at a cost of £404,000. It officially opened on 25th February 1964. In the same year the comprehensive system of education was given a boost with the election of a Labour Government which backed the policy. In January 1965 Sunderland Council decided on an all-comprehensive system of secondary education and to scrap the 11 plus.

Model School

I went to Red House Comprehensive between 1966 to 1971. As it was one of the first comprehensives in the country the headmaster, Ken Dyos, wanted to make the school a model for others to follow. To make it the best I think he tried to base Red House on the public school system.

You were not allowed on to the tennis courts unless you wore all white. Rich kids with all the gear could play to their heart's content. The problem was that they were useless. Perhaps this is one of the reasons why Britain does not produce Wimbledon champions. Winners might come from hungry 'poor' kids.

I think they would have preferred it as a rugby-playing school. I remember one year there was not enough boys willing to turn out for the school rugby team. The school threatened to scrap the football team unless enough boys agreed to turn out for the rugby eleven.

While it was commendable to try to aspire to the best for its pupils, such as Speech Days at the Empire Theatre, many of the things had little relevance to an almost exclusively working class community.

Mark Taylor

Below: Red House Comprehensive still going strong after more than thirty years.

Successful Red House teams at the annual school presentation in 1982.

If Castletown is the 'hotbed' of football Red House is certainly 'warm'. *Right:* England Schoolboy internationals Tony Nesbit *(right)* and Tony Philliskirk outside Red House Comp. Both lads went on to play League football. On leaving school Tony Nesbit signed for Newcastle United and was in the same team as Paul Gascoigne which lifted the FA Youth Cup. He went on to make his full debut for United. Tony Philliskirk signed for Sheffield United in 1983 and his goalscoring talents later took him to Rotherham, Oldham, Preston and Bolton.

Another former Red House pupil who went on to a career as a professional footballer was Bruce Halliday. After playing for Newcastle United he appeared for Bury, Bristol City and Hereford.

In 1983-84 Red House Comprehensive had the best school football team in the country. In the Final of the English Schools' FA Trophy at Roker Park they thrashed Stanground School from Peterborough 6-0. On their way to the Final they beat teams from Cleveland, Merseyside, Leicestershire and Sunderland (Southmoor).

Top and right: Action from the Final at Roker Park.

Below: The triumphant Red house team with the English Schools' FA Trophy. The first Sunderland school to lift England's top competition.

Of the outstanding Red House team that won the trophy no less than four signed for League clubs: Tony Nesbit, Ian Chandler, Kevin Jobling and David Dodsworth.

Chandler played for Barnsley, Stockport and Aldershot. Jobling played for Leicester before moving to Grimsby. Dodsworth was also at Filbert Street but was homesick and returned to Sunderland. For many he was one of the best of the Red House Cup-winning side and appeared certain to make the grade.

St Thomas Aquinas

When St Thomas Aquinas RC Secondary School first opened it was separated into a boys school and girls school. In September 1962, 450 boys became the first pupils followed eighteen months later by 270 girls.

St Thomas Aquinas closed in 1987 and its pupils transferred to St Anthony's and St Aidan's. Today the old school buildings house the City of Sunderland College's Hylton Centre *(above).*

Football Stars

Like its neighbour Red House Comprehensive, St Thomas Aquinas had a strong footballing tradition. The school had two of their pupils in the same England Schoolboy team in 1971-72. Wilf Rostron and Peter Stronach both appeared in all eight of England's games that season. Two of their teammates in the St Thomas Aquinas side - the Callaghan twins Tom and David - also played for Durham County. All four joined Sunderland AFC (Wilf Rostron via Arsenal).

Sunday Best

Above: Red House Workmen's Club with an impressive display of silverware. Over the last decade the club's Sunday football team have been the best in Sunderland. In 1992 Red House became the first Sunderland CIU League side to win the Durham Sunday Cup and then went on to retain the cup the following season. Secretary John Wake hopes the next decade is just as successful.

RIVERSIDE & NORTH HYLTON ROAD

The Ericsson (later Plessey) Factory at North Hylton Road.

Jimmy Connor

Jimmy Connor

For generations Connor's newsagents on North Hylton Road has served the local community. Jimmy Connor was one of Sunderland' greatest footballers before the war. The Scottish international winger was forced into early retirement after a bad knee injury. Stan Reid recalls Jimmy was a true gentleman.

The Torrens public house on North Hylton Road. It took its name from a famous Sunderland-built clipper of the last century. The *Torrens* was one of the fastest vessels sailing between England and Australia and the famous novelist Joseph Conrad served on the ship for a number of years.

Bradford-based car component manufacturers Hepworth and Grandage moved to Sunderland in the early 1960s. Lord Hailsham performed the opening ceremony at the factory on 28th June 1963. Within eighteen months the 750 workforce were producing one million piston rings a week. Now called AE Goetze Automotive Ltd the foundry is still one of Wearside's biggest employers today.

Much like today, in the 1960s various agencies built factories on Wearside then once completed looked for occupants. The Board of Trade had a factory constructed on North Hylton Road then tried to fill it. In 1965 London-based Olin Mathieson moved into the factory that had stood empty for a year after completion. The building is now occupied by Cowies (Arriva).

Homeworthy Furniture are another large employer on North Hylton Road. Since the 1970s it has grown into one of the biggest furniture manufacturers in the region.

The new retail park at Castletown. In recent years the riverside from Southwick to Castletown has been transformed. Offices, shopping outlets and small business units have regenerated the area.

Ericsson

Ericsson moved into a factory on North Hylton Road in 1946 where they made and assembled telephone parts.

Soon the workforce at the factory had passed the one thousand mark. A large proportion of these were women who came from the neighbouring estates.

The finished products were made for both the home and export market. Even before Ericsson set up on Wearside they supplied the local Post Office with telephone equipment. In 1954 the company won a big contract to build automatic telephone exchanges in Quebec, Canada.

In 1962 an extension to Ericssons doubled the size of the plant and took the workforce to over two thousand.

Right: An advert for Ericsson's North Hylton Road factory in 1950.

Below: Women workers at Ericsson.

A Telephone System for every Establishment

A Telephone Instrument for every Purpose

TELECOMMUNICATION EQUIPMENT

USED BY GOVERNMENT DEPARTMENTS, MUNICIPAL AUTHORITIES AND PRIVATE UNDERTAKINGS EVERYWHERE, BECAUSE IT IS

EFFICIENT AND DEPENDABLE

PART OF THE ERICSSON MODERN FACTORY AT

SOUTHWICK, SUNDERLAND

Telephone : SUNDERLAND 3888

Write for details of our

PRIVATE AUTOMATIC EXCHANGES

SUPPLIED ON EASY RENTAL TERMS WHICH INCLUDE FULL MAINTENANCE

HEAD OFFICE:

22 LINCOLN'S INN FIELDS, LONDON, W.C.2

Telephones : HOLborn 6936 (5 lines)

Telegrams : ERICLOND, LONDON

By the mid-1960s Plessey owned the factory and continued making telecommunications equipment. *Above:* Plessey assembly workers around 1970. At its peak the factory employed 3,500 people. As one of Sunderland's biggest employers it was a shock when redundancies began in the spring of 1977. When Plessey closed it was a hammer blow to the local economy with the loss of so many wage-earners.

The Plessey Factory in its heyday. After its closure part of the Plessey plant was demolished and the remainder used as small business units.

Timber Beach Nature Reserve

Timber Beach Nature Reserve lies on the riverside between North Hylton and Southwick. This inland salt marsh is the most northerly on the east coast. It supports a wide range of plant and wildlife.

Birds such as oystercatchers, cormorants, sandpipers, ringed plovers and red shanks can be seen. The plant community include seablite, glasswort, sea clubrush and reed beds. As the river has become less polluted in recent years salmon, sea trout and brown trout have reappeared. In the last days of the shipyards men on night shift were known to take a salmon or two.

Decline of Fish Stocks

At one time salmon and trout were plentiful in the river. There used to be a long deep pool at Park's Nook (opposite Claxheugh Rock). This was as much as 20 feet below the present river bed and allowed fish to rest before making their way up stream. Illegal dumping of ballast led to these deep shelters for fish filling up. One of the sites ballast should have been off loaded was Robert Reay's land at North Hylton. Many keels did not reach their destination, instead they jettisoned their loads of sand in the deep pools. This in turn affected the fish stocks in the river.

While this may have contributed to the disappearance of fish in the Wear the main culprit was industrialisation. Effluent and waste from sewers, factories, collieries and chemical works all helped pollute the river.

Wood for shipbuilding at Timber Beach in the summer of 1886.

Nature Reserve

A map showing the Nature Reserve at Timber Beach in 1980.

Wessington Way which runs parallel to the River Wear is only a short distance from the tranquility of the reserve.

Plans for a sports complex for Austin & Pickersgill nearby were shelved. Just over a decade later the shipyard itself was closed.

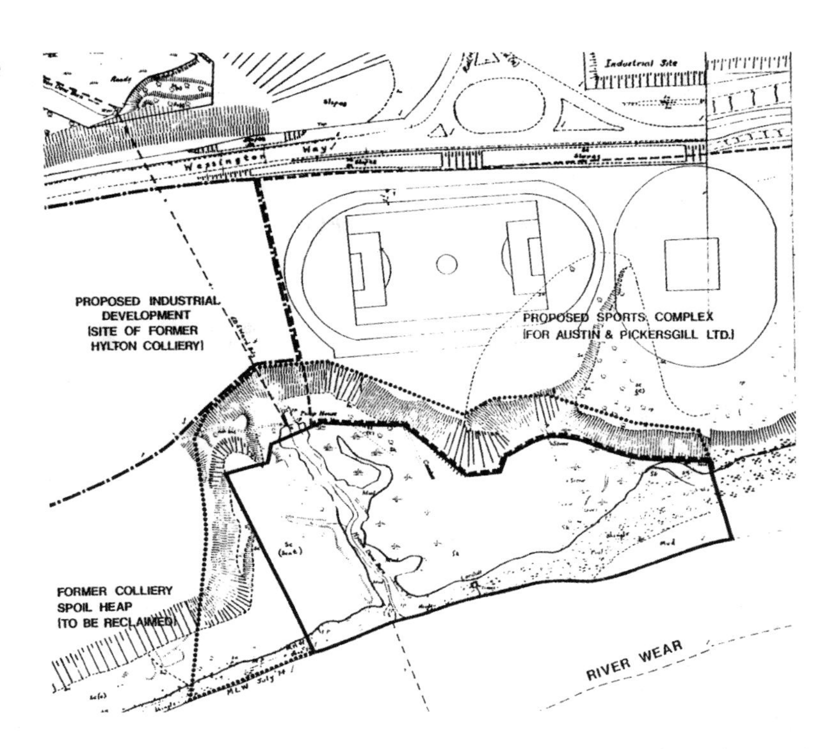

Timber Beach Today

Concrete Ships

The Wear Concrete Building Company set up a yard on the Saltgrass between Southwick and Castletown to build concrete ships. Ferro-concrete was seen as an alternative to steel in shipyards during the First World War. In early 1918 work began on laying the berths and building offices and workshops. By the summer of 1918 the firm employed 100 men at the yard. These included: shipwrights, joiners, steel benders and labourers. The first vessel was not launched until 1919 after the war had ended. This was the concrete sea-going tug *Cretehawser*. This vessel can still be seen in the Wear only a short distance from where she was launched. Other tugs and barges followed but the idea of concrete ships never caught on.

Above: The *Cretehawser* in 1990 with reclamation work on the old Hylton Colliery site taking place in the background. The River Wear Commissioners bought the 260 ton *Cretehawser* and her sister ship *Cretestem* for use in emergency if the harbour installations were damaged. During the last war the tugs were hit in an air-raid and the *Cretehawser* was eventually towed up river to her final resting place. *Below:* The *Cretehawser* lying derelict today.

MARLEY POTS

The entrance to Marley Pots playing fields.

Pre-War Building

In 1931 Sunderland Council agreed to build 154 four-roomed houses at Marley Pots. Messrs W.D. & R. Allison of Whitburn won the contract to build the houses for the sum of £63,170. After a request from the Ministry of Health to reduce the area of four-roomed houses the Council revised its plans. At Marley Pots it would now build 104 four-roomed and 50 three-roomed houses. The Council did reject another request from the Ministry to omit mangle sheds from new houses.

The financial outlay did not end at the cost of building houses. Roads (£5,000), sewers (£2,900) and paving stones (£1,900) all contributed to the final bill for the Marley Pots Estate.

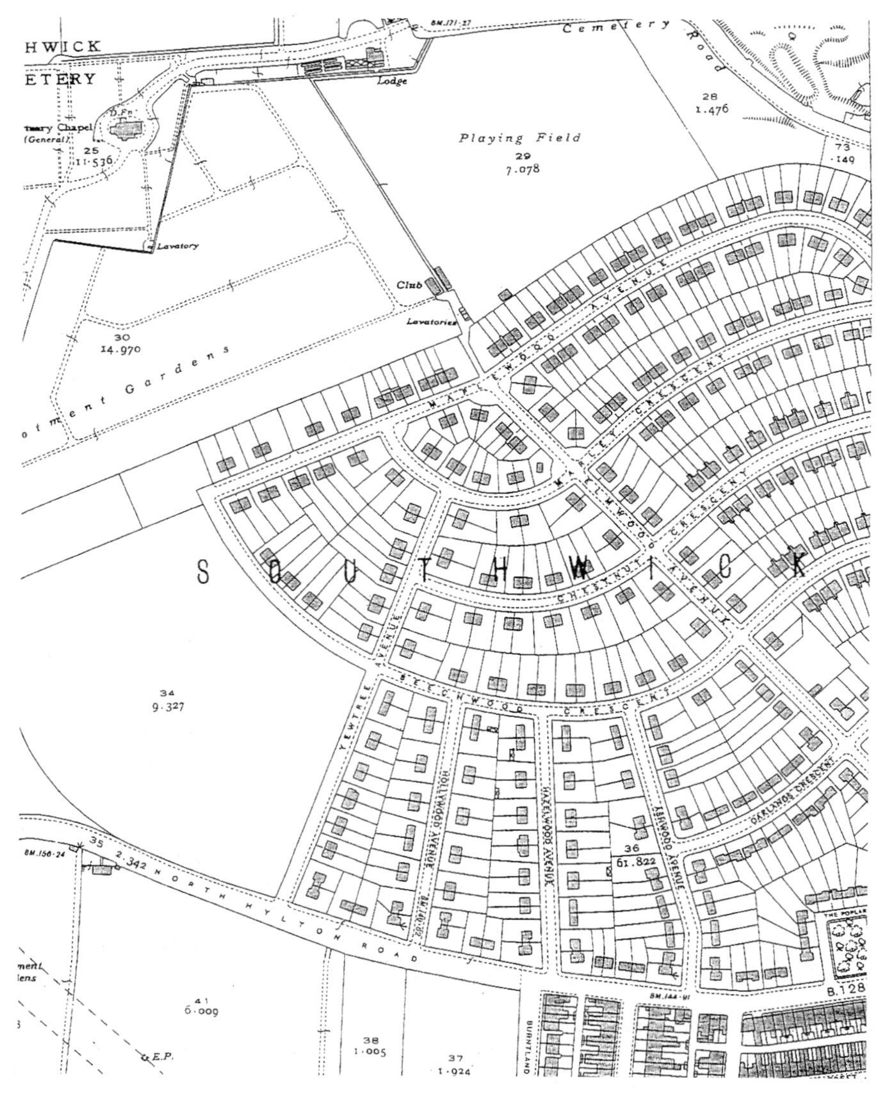

A map of Marley Pots shortly after the estate was built.

Marley Pots

Marley stone is a type of limestone that was quarried in this area. Marley stone was used by local farmers to repair their roadways. Deep holes dug in limestone districts were known as Pots.

Brave New World

Sunderland Annual Report of the Medical Officer of Health in 1936 gave the results of a survey carried out on families who moved from slum areas to the new estates built on green field sites. One fifth of the survey were living on Marley Pots Estate.

The vast majority of families were satisfied with the change. This is reflected in some of their additional remarks:

Better health and appetites. Children improved and love the bath. Healthier and garden helpful. Better house and plenty of good air. Every conveniences, would not go back, house inspires to do best.

However, there was a down side to these new estates built on the edge of town. Many elderly people could not settle and yearned for their old neighbourhoods. The higher rents were a burden on family budgets, as were the higher heating costs for the bigger houses and travelling expenses. The bigger appetites also put a strain on family purse strings.

Maplewood Avenue today.

Price of Housing

In the 1930s the first residents of Marley Pots were more than happy with their new houses. However, there were complaints about the higher rents. On average the rents for houses in old parts of town were 5/6¾d but in the new housing developments rents were 9/6½d per week. While the amenities in houses on the green field sites were far superior to those in run down areas, like the East End, the rent increases were a big drain on the household budget.

Marley Pots today, the sixty-year-old estate has undergone radical renovation in recent years.

Football fields at Marley Pots. Recently the site has been landscaped with trees.

Summerbell's Allotments

Summerbell's Allotments near Southwick Cemetery today. Before the First World War Thomas Summerbell was one of the town's Members of Parliament and his eldest son Thomas was later a local councillor. In 1935 Thomas Jnr became Sunderland's first socialist mayor.

A cartoon from the *Football Echo* of Maplewood S.C. in the 1950-51 season. At this time the team played in the First Division of the Wearside Combination League. Many of the residents of this area at the top of Marley Pots came from the East End.

Marley Pots Playcentre. Marley Pots Boxing Club is based at the centre with training sessions three times a week.

Match at Marley Pots

A match at Marley Pots on 4th October 1997 between Aquatic Sports and The Robin. This Wearside Combination Premiership League game ended in a 3-1 victory to Aquatic. Marley Pots is the home pitch of Aquatic whose management refer to the ground as the San Siro (Milan).

The Salvation Army building at Maplewood Avenue was built forty years ago to serve the local community.

Marley Pots has remained a distinctive community since the 1930s. Despite their houses adjoining Southwick the residents of Marley Pots have retained their own unique character.

SECTION TEN

WITHERWACK

Albert Anderson of Witherwack surrounded by pictures of local cinemas on which he has written extensively.

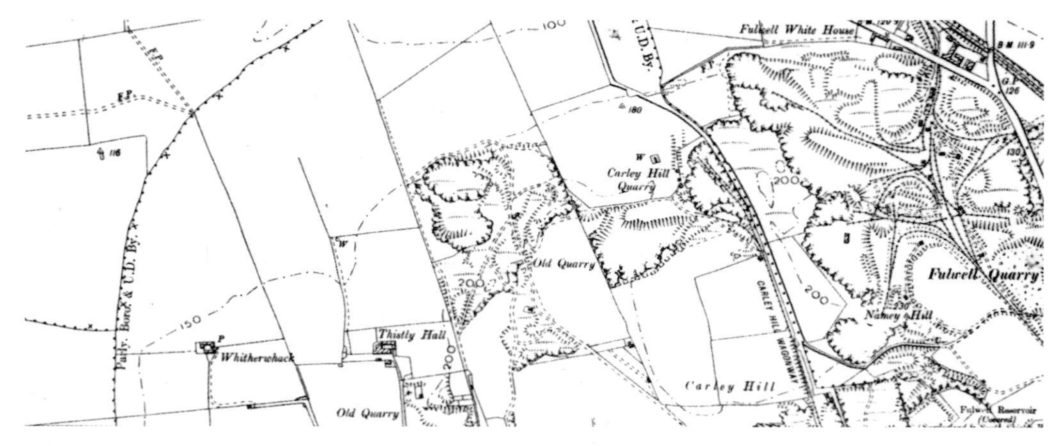

A map showing 'Whitherwhack' Farm in the last century. The farm stood on the site of the estate that now bears its name. It appears the farm was named after *wither* - willows, which once grew nearby and *whack* - share, portion, allowance, dividing up or alternatively it could be a variant of *wic* - outlying farm or premises used for special purposes.

Witherwack Farm

In the 1890s Scotsman Charles Dunn was the occupant of Witherwack Farm. He lived there with his Northumberland-born wife and nine children. Two teenage girls worked as domestic servants in the farmhouse.

Thistle Hall

In the last century the spelling of place names varied considerably. In the 1851 Census William Smithson farmed 60 acres at 'Thistle' Hall. By the time William and Mary Humble farmed there in the 1880s it was down as 'Thisley' Hall. A decade later it was recorded as 'Thistley' Hall.

A view looking along Wembley Road, in the distance is Marley Pots football fields.

Above: A special treat for children to the Odeon cinema in January 1978 organised by the Thistle Club.

At a meeting of local residents at Carley Hill School in the late '60s it was decided a new social club should be built. This would be called the Thistle Club. The name was a compromise because the club would be sited between Witherwack and Carley Hill. A new estate was planned at the time and this would have been called the Thistle Hall Estate.

Below: The Thistle Club was renamed The Dagmar in the early '80s. The present name owes more to TV's *Eastenders* than to local history.

Witherwack Primary School

Throughout the 1970s Witherwack School had one of the finest football teams in the town. They won the Topliff Cup (for Sunderland's smaller schools) on six successive occasions between 1972-73 to 1977-78. Remarkably in two of these seasons Witherwack also won the Ditchburn Cup (for all Sunderland schools).

Alan Hunter, Head Teacher at Witherwack School was President of Sunderland & District Primary Schools' Association from 1975 to 1991.

Ian Chandler is one of Witherwack's old boys who went on to play League football. He joined Barnsley in 1986 and went on to turn out for Stockport County and Aldershot.

Tongue Twister

The name Witherwack took some getting used to for a few of the older generation. I was in the town one day when an old lady asked me where the bus stop for 'Wicky Wack' was.

Albert Anderson

Houses continue to be built on the estate, these are going up next to Witherwack School.

Albert Anderson *(right)* at the opening of the Screen on the River at the University of Sunderland's St Peter's Campus. Tyneside Cinema Director Briony Hanson *(left)* and Professor Flavia Swann of the University's School of Arts, Design & Communications accompany Albert at the launch of Sunderland's newest cinema in 1995.

Albert Anderson is one of Witherwack's most famous residents. He is author of a number of books on Sunderland, these include *The Dream Palaces of Sunderland* and *A Century of Sunderland Cinemas.* Born on the Barbary Coast (Monkwearmouth), Albert had the ideal job to satisfy his passion for the pictures - for years he was a projectionist at the Roker Variety Theatre.

The New Estate

The *Southwick District Plan* in 1967 reported work had started on housing at Witherwack. A total of 783 houses would be built on the estate by 1980.

Left: Houses in the estate's Wiltshire Road

Tatie Picking

Potatoes were an important crop for farms from North Hylton in the west to Witherwack and Carley Hill in the east. This was a cheap food for the ever growing population of Sunderland.

At harvest time a great number of people were employed to gather in the potatoes. There was always a willing force of part-time potato pickers, wanting to supplement their wages and take home a sack of potatoes from gleaning the field. As harvest time coincided with schools' half-term children often did this backbreaking work. Women were another source of labour.

Lady Shearers

Ladies were also engaged in other types of agricultural work. John Thompson in *Old Monkwearmouth & Its Surroundings* recalled how from the 1820s the Wheatsheaf Inn, Broad Street (now Roker Avenue) was where farmers could hire seasonal workers. A robust class of women known as 'Shearers' used the pub as a rendezvous. 'With their sickle or hook in hand they could be seen, during the harvest season, waiting to be engaged by farmers to cut down their grain crops.'

Youngsters on their way home from gleaning potatoes in the late 1950s. Most of these Monkwearmouth lads moved up to Town End Farm when it was built.

CARLEY HILL

A Coastal Watch Mirror for detecting Zeppelins in the First World War.

Carley Hill

Carley Hill is part of a limestone plateau which covers the Sunderland area. On the other side of the river Building Hill, Hasting Hill and Tunstall Hill are all part of this same rock formation.

Some of Carley Hill's blocks of flats have been radically renovated in recent years. Earls Court is one example of these changes.

The Wearsider - Carley Hill's local.

The School That Never Was

In the mid '60s plans were made for a comprehensive school at Carley Hill but the final decision was constantly put off. When Margaret Thatcher became Minister of Education she dropped the scheme. When Labour returned to power they gave the go ahead again only to shelve the plan because of an economic crises. At a meeting of the Council in February 1975 a firm commitment to build Carley Hill Comprehensive was given. In the end the school was never built.

Carley Hill Primary School has been a 'focal point' for the local community. In the early 1970s Headmaster Mr Phillips encouraged parents into the school. Parent-teacher meetings was one of the means by which this was achieved.

Right: Eastbourne Square in the mid-1960s.

Below right: The same view in October 1997. Unlike similar blocks of flats on Carley Hill, Eastbourne Square, on the exterior at least, has not changed radically over thirty years.

Below: Edmonton Square in Carley Hill today. All the names of the streets on the estate begin with the letter E. The south of England is well represented with streets named after Elstree, Epping and Epsom. Some of the more adventurous are: Everton, Everest and Edinburgh.

Zeppelin Warning

Beside the pathway that runs from Carley Hill to Fulwell lies a little known part of Wearside's history. This concrete dish was built as an early warning system in the First World War. It was used to detect Zeppelins as they approached from over the North Sea. The sound from the airship's engines bounced off the dish onto a receiver. This gave the air defences a crucial 15 minutes to prepare to engage the enemy. The City of Sunderland recognised the historic importance of the Coastal Watch Mirror by placing a 'blue plaque' on the structure.

Above: The Rolls Royce football pitch situated on the land above Carley Hill Quarry. The Coastal Watch Mirror can just be seen at the top of the picture to the left of the goal posts.

Right: The land bordering the houses on Carley Hill is ideal pasture land for horses.

Carley Hill Limestone Quarries

Two hundred years ago the lime trade was one of the most important exports on Wearside. The limestone was transported from quarries like Carley Hill down wagonways to be burnt in kilns on the banks of the Wear. The end product was used as a fertiliser on farms, for building mortar and as a flux in the glassmaking industry.

Below: A nineteenth century map showing Carley Hill Quarry and the wagonway.

Shipping

The lime was exported to Teesside, Whitby and to Scotland. To meet this demand as many as 50 ships were employed. These vessels ranged from 40 to 100 tons which in turn kept local shipbuilders busy.

Quarrymen

The 1841 Census records John Forster and family living at Carley Hill Cottages. The head of the household and two of his sons worked at the quarry.

In the last century limestone was transported from Carley Hill Quarries to kilns on the riverside in wagons run on horse tramways.

Above and right: Today the wagonway is a public footpath.

Below: The kilns were on the riverbank opposite were the Liebherr works is today.

Romans at Carley Hill

The Romans had overrun the North by 80 AD and remained for three centuries. Hadrian's Wall and the fort at Arbeia (South Shields) are the most famous monuments to the Roman presence in the region. However, there is evidence of their stay in a number of locations on Wearside. One of these was at Carley Hill.

In 1820 a small Roman statue of Jupiter was discovered at Carley Hill Quarry. The bronze figure stands 4 1/4 inches high *(right)*.

It is thought to have been a *Lar* - a household god. Roman families placed these statues in their home for protection.

Below: Carley Hill Quarry.